ACCESS GUIDE TO

Liturgy & Worship

Edited by
John Roberto

THE WORLD OF
DON BOSCO
MULTIMEDIA

New Rochelle, NY

Access Guide to Liturgy & Worship
is published as a service for adults who love the
young and want to share the Gospel with them.

It is a guide to understanding the young and a resource
book for helping them. As such, it is addressed to
parents, parish youth ministers, clergy who work with
the young, and teachers.

Forthcoming *Access Guides*:
Justice
Leadership
Retreats
Advocacy
Families and Youth
Prayer and Spirituality

BV
178
.L58
1990

Prepared in conjunction with
The Center for Youth Ministry Development

Access Guide to Liturgy & Worship
©1990 Salesian Society, Inc. / Don Bosco Multimedia
475 North Ave., Box T, New Rochelle, NY 10802
All rights reserved

Library of Congress Cataloging-in-Publication Data
Liturgy & Worship / edited by John Roberto.
p. cm. — (Access guides to youth ministry)
Includes bibliographical references.
    1. Liturgics.   2. Youth—Religious life.   3. Worship (Religious
    education)   I. Roberto, John.   II. Title: Liturgy & Worship.   III. Series.
BV   178.L58 1990   264'.02'00835—dc20   90-41014
ISBN 0-89944-141-6 $14.95

Printed in the United States of America

9/90   9 8 7 6 5 4 3 2 1

Table of Contents

PREFACE TO THE ACCESS GUIDES

A NEW CONCEPT

Welcome to the *Access Guides to Youth Ministry* series. The Center for Youth Ministry and Don Bosco Multimedia have created the *Access Guide to Youth Ministry* series to provide leaders in ministry with youth with both the foundational understandings and the practical tools they need to create youth ministry programming for each component outlined in *A Vision of Youth Ministry*. *Access Guides* are being developed for Pop Culture, Evangelization, Leadership (Enablement), Family Life, Guidance; Justice, Peace, and Service; Liturgy and Worship, Adolescent Spirituality and Prayer, and Retreats. Each *Access Guide* provides foundational essays, processes for developing that component, and approaches and program models to use in your setting. The blend of theory and practice makes each *Access Guide* a unique resource in youth ministry. To help you understand the context for the *Access Guide* series we would like to provide you with a brief overview of the goals and components of a comprehensive approach to ministry with youth.

A RENEWED MINISTRY

Over a decade ago, Catholic Youth Ministry engaged in a process of self-reflection and analysis that resulted in a re-visioning of youth ministry — establishing the goals, principles, and components of a comprehensive, contemporary ministry with youth. *A Vision of Youth Ministry* outlined this comprehensive approach to ministry with youth and became the foundation for a national vision of Catholic Youth Ministry. In the years since the publishing of *A Vision of Youth Ministry*, Catholic Youth Ministry across the United States has experienced tremendous growth.

From the outset, the *Vision* paper made clear its ecclesial focus: "As one among many ministries of the Church, youth ministry must be understood in terms of the mission and ministry of the whole Church." (3) The focus is clearly ministerial. "The Church's mission is threefold: to proclaim the good news of salvation; offer itself as a group of people transformed by the Spirit into a community of faith, hope, and love; and to bring God's justice and love to others through service in its individual, social, and political dimensions." (3) This threefold mission formed the basis of the framework or components of youth ministry: Word (evangelization and catechesis), Worship, Community, Justice and Service, Guidance and Healing, Enablement, and Advocacy.

This threefold mission also gives youth ministry a dual focus. Youth ministry is a ministry within the community of faith — ministering to believing youth *and* to the wider society — reaching out to serve youth in our society. While the experience of the past decade has emphasized ministry *within* the community, youth ministry must also address the social situation and needs of all youth in society. A comprehensive approach demands a balance between ministry *within* the Christian community and ministry *by* the Christian community *to* young people within our society and world.

The *Vision paper* described a broad concept of ministry with youth using four dimensions. Youth Ministry is...

> *To* youth — responding to youth's varied needs
> *With* youth — working with adults to fulfill their common responsibility for the Church's mission
> *By* youth — exercising their own ministry to others: peers, community, world
> *For* youth — interpreting the needs of youth, especially in areas of injustice and acting on behalf of or with youth for a change in the systems which create injustice.

Two goals were initially developed for the Church's ministry with youth:

> Goal #1: Youth Ministry works to the total personal and spiritual growth of each young person.
> Goal #2: Youth Ministry seeks to draw young people to responsible participation in the life, mission, and work of the faith community. (7)

The first goal emphasizes *becoming* — focusing on the personal level of human existence. The second goal emphasizes *belonging* — focusing on the interpersonal or communal dimension of human existence.

In light of the Church's priority upon justice and peace, and the mission of the Church to transform society (for example, *The Challenge of Peace*, NCCB, 1983; and *Economic Justice for All*, NCCB, 1986), it would be appropriate to consider adding a *third* goal. This third goal would challenge youth ministry to empower young people to become aware of the social responsibilities of the Christian faith — the call to live and work for justice and peace. Youth ministry needs to empower young people with the knowledge and skills to transform the unjust structures of society so that these structures promote justice, respect human dignity, promote human rights, and build peace. This third goal emphasizes *transforming* — focusing on the public or social structural level of human existence and giving a greater comprehensiveness to youth ministry.

> Goal #3: Youth Ministry empowers young people to transform the world as disciples of Jesus Christ by living and working for justice and peace.

An underdeveloped, but increasingly important, section of the Vision paper is the contexts of youth ministry. "In all places, youth ministry occurs within a given social, cultural, and religious context which shapes the specific form of the ministry." This contextual approach seeks to view young people as part of a number of social systems which impact on their growth, values, and faith, rather than as isolated individuals. Among these systems are the family, society, the dominant culture, youth culture, ethnic culture, school, and local church community. In the last several years, youth ministry has become much more aware of the impact of these systems.

A COMPREHENSIVE APPROACH

The framework (or components) describes distinct aspects for developing a comprehensive, integrated ministry with youth. Briefly, these components include:

Evangelization — reaching out to young people who are uninvolved in the life of the community and inviting them into a relationship with Jesus and the Christian community. Evangelization involves proclaiming the Good News of Jesus through programs and relationships.

Catechesis — promoting a young person's growth in Christian faith through the kind of teaching and learning that emphasizes understanding, reflection, and transformation. This is accomplished through systematic, planned, and intentional programming (curriculum). (See The Challenge of Adolescent Catechesis).

Prayer and Worship — assisting young people in deepening their relationship with Jesus through the development of a personal prayer life; and providing a variety of prayer and worship experiences with youth to deepen and celebrate their relationship with Jesus in a caring Christian community; involving young people in the sacramental life of the Church.

Community Life — building Christian community with youth through programs and relationships which promote openness, trust, valuing the person, cooperation, honesty, taking responsibility, and willingness to serve; creating a climate where young people can grow and share their struggles, questions, and joys with other youth and adults; helping young people feel like a valued part of the global Church.

Guidance and Healing — providing youth with sources of support and counsel as they face personal problems and pressures (for example, family problems, peer pressure, substance abuse, suicide) and decide on careers and important life decisions; providing appropriate support and guidance for youth during times of stress and crisis; helping young people deal with the problems they face and the pressures people place on them; developing a better understanding of their parents and learning how to communicate with them.

Justice, Peace, and Service — guiding young people in developing a Christian social consciousness and a commitment to a life of justice and peace through educational programs and service/action involvement; infusing the concepts of justice and peace into all youth ministry relationships and programming.

Enablement — developing, supporting, and utilizing the leadership abilities and personal gifts of youth and adults in youth ministry, empowering youth for ministry with their peers; developing a leadership team to organize and coordinate the ministry with youth.

Advocacy — interpreting the needs of youth: personal, family, and social especially in areas of injustices towards or oppression of youth, and acting with or on behalf of youth for a change in the systems which create injustice; giving young people a voice and empowering them to address the social problems that they face.

WORKS CITED

The Challenge of Adolescent Catechesis. Washington, DC: NFCYM Publications, 1986.

A Vision of Youth Ministry. Washington, DC: USCC, Department of Education, 1976.

ABOUT THE AUTHORS

John Roberto is director of the Center for Youth Ministry Development. He is the managing editor of the joint publishing project between the Center and Don Bosco Multimedia and the co-editor of *Access Guides to Youth Ministry: Evangelization*. He holds an M.A. in Religious Education from Fordham University.

Walter Brueggemann is professor of Old Testament at Eden Theological Seminary in St. Louis. He holds a doctorate in theology from Union Theological Seminary in New York. Among his published works are *Praying the Psalms, The Bible Makes Sense, Prophetic Imagination, and To Act Justly, Love Tenderly, Walk Humbly*.

Michael Downey is assistant professor of theology at Loyola Marymount University in Los Angeles. In addition to a doctorate in theology, he holds a master's degree in special education. He is the author of *Clothed in Christ* and *A Blessed Weakness: The Spirit of Jean Vanier and l'Arche*.

Kathleen Fischer teaches theology at Seattle University. She holds a doctorate in theology from the Graduate Theological Union in Berkeley, California. She is the author of *The Inner Rainbow — The Imagination in Christian Life*.

Edward Foley, OFM Cap., is assistant professor of liturgy at the Catholic Theological Union in Chicago.

Gilbert Ostdiek, OFM, teaches liturgy at the Catholic Theological Union in Chicago. He holds an STD degree in theology and is author of *Catechesis for Liturgy*, as well as numerous articles on liturgy and sacramental theology.

Michael Moynahan, SJ, is founder of the Berkeley Liturgical Drama Guild. He holds a doctorate in theology from the Jesuit School of Theology at Berkeley. He has given workshops nationally and internationally on the dramatic arts. He is the author of *God of Untold Tales, How the Word Became Flesh*, and *Once Upon a Parable*.

Janet Schaffran is campus minister at Walsh College, Canton, Ohio. **Pat Kozak** is a graduate student at Pacific School of Religion in Berkeley, California. They are co-authors of *More Than Words — Prayer and Ritual for Inclusive Communities*.

Mark Searle is associate director of the Notre Dame Center for Pastoral Liturgy and professor of theology at the University of Notre Dame. He holds a doctorate in theology and a diploma in liturgical studies. He is editor of the review Assembly. He has authored *The Making of Christians and Liturgy Made Simple*.

Thomas N. Tomaszek has been a consultant in youth ministry for the Archdiocese of Milwaukee for eight years; He holds a Masters of Education from the University of Wisconsin and a Masters in Theological Studies from St. Francis School of Pastoral Ministry in Milwaukee. He has also created the innovative Music and Liturgy Institute for the annual Region Seven Youth University.

John H. Westerhoff, III, is professor of religion and education at Duke University Divinity School and former editor of Religious Education. He is a worldwide lecturer and author of more than fifteen books, including *Will our Children Have Faith?*, *Generation to Generation*, and *Living the Faith Community*.

ACKNOWLEDGEMENTS

"What is Liturgy?" by Mark Searle is reprinted with permission of Liturgical Press from *Liturgy Made Simple*, Collegeville: Liturgical Press, 1981.

"Sacraments and Christian Living" by Michael Downey is reprinted with permission of Crossroads Publishing from *Clothed in Christ*, New York: Crossroads, 1987.

"Liturgy: A High Risk Invitation" by Walter Brueggemann is reprinted with permission from the Spring 1986 issue of *Reformed Liturgy and Music*, published by the Office of Worship for the Presbyterian Church (U.S.A.), 1044 Alta Vista Road, Louisville, KY 40205.

"Rituals for Adolescence" by John H. Westerhoff,III, first appeared as "Betwixt and Between" and is reprinted with permission from the September 1977 issue of *Liturgy*, published by the Liturgical Conference, 1017 12th St. NW, Washington, DC 20005.

"Qualities and Criteria for Liturgical Celebrations" by Gilbert Ostdiek, OFM, is reprinted with permission of The Pastoral Press from *Catechesis for Liturgy*, Washington, D.C.: The Pastoral Press, 1986.

"Liturgical Drama" by Michael Moynahan, SJ, is reprinted with permission of Paulist Press from edited by John Mossi, New York: Paulist Press, 1976.

"Guidelines for Reading Scripture" by Kathleen Fischer is excerpted from "Imagination and Scripture" with permission of Paulist Press from *The Inner Rainbow*, New York: Paulist Press, 1983.

"Symbols and Rituals," "Cultural Pluralism," and "Inclusive Language" are reprinted with permission of Meyer-Stone Books from *More Than Words* by Janet Schaffran and Pat Kozak, Oak Park: Meyer-Stone Books, 1988.

"An Overview of the Communal Rites of Penance" by Edward Foley, OFM Cap., is a condensed version of "Communal Rites of Penance: Insights and Options" reprinted with permission of Liturgical Press from *Reconciliation: The Continuing Agenda*, edited by Robert J. Kennedy, Collegeville: Liturgical Press, 1987.

Part I

Understanding Liturgy & Worship

Overview

The Church's sacramental and liturgical life provides opportunities for nurturing a deeper relationship with Jesus Christ in our young people and in fostering a deeper involvement of young people in the life of the Christian community. This rich variety of worship experiences also provides a very important way for young people to celebrate and express *their* faith — in symbols, rituals, music, art, drama. Young people need to celebrate and express their faith through the community's worship *and* through their own worship experiences. This is an integral element of the faith maturing process. It is a task that everyone in ministry with youth must address.

Access Guides to Youth Ministry: Liturgy and Worship takes on this challenge. In Part One of this book, the foundational understandings so essential to a well informed liturgical practice with youth are developed. Part Two of this book provides you with the guidelines, processes, and key elements for preparing liturgical and worship experiences with youth.

Mark Searle begins Part One by sketching the broad lines of an understanding of Church and liturgy growing out of Vatican II and offering his own overview of a theology of liturgy. His essay concludes with five general principles that can offer a basis for continued reflection, especially when we are engaged in preparing liturgies. These principles are 1) liturgy is never perfect; 2) liturgy does not always have to be different; 3) liturgy is prayer; 4) liturgy is not so much a celebration of life-as-we-know-it as it is a celebration of the mystery of life we hardly suspect; and 5) liturgy is service — both to our service of God and to God's service of us.

Michael Downey offers a very helpful essay on the intrinsic connection between sacramental celebration and Christian living. He asks what are the forms of liturgy and Christian life appropriate to our own day? To answer this question, he examines the renewed understandings of Jesus Christ, the Church, and the human person that have emerged in the latter part of the twentieth century. These changes account for the different shape our form of worship has taken after Vatican

II. He draws out the importance of giving great attention to the practical implications of what is believed and expressed in worship. Our worship must give expression to the renewed understandings.

Walter Brueggemann explores the real risks of true worship by providing a cultural and social analysis of the context of our community worship. He challenges us to believe that "the world in which we live is not a given, but a contrivance." We take this contrived world for granted; we accept it as real. It is a world that is powerfully communicated to us through the media. He writes that the real task of the Church's liturgy is to liberate people from this contrived world by offering an alternative construct of the world which is mediated through different narratives and metaphors, which provides and legitimates an alternative imagination.

Tom Tomaszek focuses our attention on worship and youth by analyzing and addressing four common problems: 1) our liturgies don't attend to youth; 2) our youth don't attend liturgy; 3) our liturgies don't speak to the signs of the times; and 4) we need liturgical formation. He uses four movements of love (take, bless, break, give) to frame his response to the four problems. Tomaszek concludes his essay with nineteen suggestions for improving worship for youth.

John Westerhoff analyzes rituals for adolescence by first examining the concept of adolescence using several faith-style descriptions of faith development: affiliative, searching, and owned faith. He then examines the nature of ritual in today's world and then distinguishes between rites of the community (for example, Eucharist), and rites of life crisis (including rites of identity or initiation). From his analysis, he concludes that 1) adolescents share with all a need for intergenerational rites of community; 2) adolescents have significant life events that need to be celebrated; and 3) adolescents need a new identity ritual in adolescence which he calls a discipleship rite.

Chapter 1

What is Liturgy?

By Mark Searle

Before discussing the details of specific rites, it might be helpful to establish a coherent picture of the liturgy of the Church. We hardly need to be told what the liturgy is, because we already know. It is rather like the man who was asked whether he believed in infant baptism. "No," he answered, "I've seen it." But the problem is this: when he saw baptism, what did he see? There is an old and familiar story about four blind men who were introduced to an elephant. Later, as they discussed their experience, they violently disagreed about what they had encountered. An elephant, claimed the first man, who had put his arms around the elephant's leg, is a kind of tree: a very large kind of tree is what an elephant is. No, argued the second man, an elephant is a kind of snake with a very coarse skin and a strange, soft mouth. He had, of course, grasped the elephant's trunk. The third man had felt the elephant's ear and swore black and blue that an elephant was a sail on a ship. The fourth man, who had grabbed the elephant's tail, was utterly convinced that an elephant was a piece of old rope.

DIVERGENCE OF VIEWS

Similarly, people have very different and often quite conflicting views on liturgy. This makes the celebration of the liturgy somewhat problematic. Mention the word "Mass" and some people think of quiet moments in a dark church with the priest afar off quietly muttering the words of ancient Latin and moving gently through the rote of time-hallowed ritual. Others think of guitars and joyful noises, of exuberance and movement and banners and enthusiastic congregations. Others think of a small gathering of friends and neighbors in someone's home for a careful reading of the Scriptures, for spontaneous prayer, and for intimate sharing of the one bread and the one cup. Others think of the Mass in terms of solemn ritual and beautiful music, a liturgy of pomp and circumstance, speaking of a concern to put the best of human gifts and talents at the service of worshipping the transcendent God. For others still, Mass is something you have to attend if you are a Catholic: just that and no more.

Obviously, all of these different views of the Mass lead to different ideas and expectations about what should and should not be. The same is true, of course, for the four men who met the elephant: it would be unwise to put any one of them in charge of the elephant house! The problem with the liturgy, however, is not that we are blind, or that any of these images of the Mass is entirely wrong. The problem is that the liturgy, like the Church itself, is a living mystery. That is, the liturgy, like the Church, is always more than we can say, and it eludes any easy definition. Yet most of us, on the basis of our experience or religious training, have a sort of working definition or an operational image in terms of which we naturally tend to judge liturgies as good or bad, agreeable or disagreeable.

The same is, of course, true of the Church: we all have our working definitions and we respond accordingly. The *National Catholic Reporter* has a different image of Church than does *The Wanderer*. Dutch theologians — or some of them — have a different idea of what the Church is, and thus ought to be, than does the Pope. Different images of the Church create different sets of expectations and different ways of evaluating developments in the Church, whether the issue be the ordination of women or the Church's involvement in politics or the direction of ecumenism.

These kinds of disputes are not limited to the national and international scene; they percolate down into the parishes, creating tension and conflict. And it is in the parish that the liturgy is celebrated. Laws may be made in Rome, books may be written in Europe, directives may be issued from Washington, talks may be given at Notre Dame, but it is in a particular parish on a Sunday morning that out of all these rubrics and directives and bright ideas a community has to come to common worship, finding itself gathered together in the Spirit of Jesus before the presence of the Father. There the arguments have to cease — or at least be suspended — and common prayer has to rise up before the throne of God. Decisions have to be made on how we can all celebrate together, and this implies some basic common understanding of what it is we are all about. Celebrating this liturgy requires some consensus on what liturgy is for and what it means to be Church.

In this essay, therefore, I will sketch the broad lines of an understanding of Church and liturgy which might help make sense of the liturgy and offer some sense of direction in its planning. It must be remembered, however, that we are dealing with a mystery when we are engaged with the Church and the liturgy. We are dealing with something which can never be completely understood or adequately defined, for it is always open to fresh insight and deeper understanding. I offer this sketch, then, not because it is the right one and all others are wrong, but simply to serve as a point of common reference for discussion. Much more needs to be said, but this can serve as a starting point: one that is as true as I can make it to the vision of Church and liturgy given to us in the Second Vatican Council.

THE CHURCH

One of the major considerations which prompted Pope John XXIII to summon the bishops of the world to Rome for the Council was the realization that the developments of modern history had led to a profound change of awareness about the Church and the world. We were in a new situation which raised new pastoral and theological questions. This situation had to be appraised and we had to look to our Tradition for fresh sources in responding to it.

Perhaps this new awareness of the Church's situation in the world can be most dramatically summarized in the use of an image. (Segundo) If the whole history of humanity were scaled down to eight hours, the two thousand years of the Church's history would be represented by only the last couple of minutes. For most of its history, the human race has lived without the presence of the Church and its gospel in its midst. Moreover, even in the time that the Church has existed, it has never represented the religion of the majority of the human race. This has never really struck home until this century. Previously, Christians believed the world to be more or less evangelized. Of course, in the world as they saw it, there were always some who had still to be converted: underdeveloped people on the fringes of the world and a few recusant Jews in the midst of Christendom. But this was the world as they saw it; they were either ignorant of, or blind to, the existence of whole races and cultures living outside that world — peoples they had hardly discovered, living in the Americas and the Far East, in northern wastes and in the antipodes. Only in this century have we really come to full, global awareness of the extent and diversity of the human family. Only in this century have we come to realize, with something of a sense of shock, that most people on this earth have never been members of the Church and that even today, when Christianity is the most populous religion, its adherents still represent a minority of the human race.

This realization leads us to a more humble estimate of the success of Christianity and its role in history. It forces us to question the truth of our assertion that without faith and baptism no one can be saved. (Theisen) Either God's plan was somewhat wider than we had imagined it, or else it was rather late coming into effect, or not very successful in its implementation. The small percentage of Christians in the world raises all sorts of questions, not only about how the unbaptized can be saved outside the Church, but about the Church itself. If people can be saved outside the Church, i.e., if God can bring them to life with himself without the waters of baptism, then what is the Church for? If the Church is not absolutely necessary for salvation, what is it for at all?

This new self-realization of the Church's place in human history has led to a new self-image for the Church. Instead of thinking of itself as the only gateway to God, it has come increasingly to see itself as a sign established by God among the nations of the earth: a sign set up in history to show what God has done and is doing for the whole human race, whether he does it visibly or hiddenly.

What is this work of God in human history? It can perhaps best be summed up in the word "reconciliation." God is reconciling the world to himself by overcoming whatever is not of God. God is healing divisions, establishing justice where injustice rules, giving hope to the hopeless, light to the confused, peace to those who are at odds, and support to those whom hurt and fear have turned in upon themselves. In short, the word of God is God's victory over sin and the establishment of the Kingdom when evil would enslave us.

This new order is coming about, not only in individual hearts, but in the human community itself. Thus, through the action of the Holy Spirit, the Kingdom — or rule — of God can spring up at any time and in any place: in a Chinese commune, an Indian village, a Russian factory, a Jewish kibbutz, an Arab family, an inner-city ghetto — wherever, and however fitfully, God's gracious and healing presence overcomes the power of evil. When the mistrust of neighbors is overcome in friendship, when an addict is helped to escape addiction, when a stranger finds welcome, when a person refuses to spread malicious gossip, when a mother by her unconditional love helps her child grow more self-confident and generous, when a nation takes a risk for peace — whenever such things happen there is the presence of God's Spirit, the power of his salvation, and the blossoming of his Kingdom.

The Church is to be a sign to the world of the word of God: not a signpost pointing somewhere else, but a sign, a manifestation, of what God is doing here for all. The Church is a community of people called to recognize and cooperate with that work of God. The Church is a community of believers whose faith is expressed in the acknowledgement of praise and prayer as well as in the acknowledgement that is expressed by putting one's life at the service of the Kingdom of God for the salvation of one's neighbors. The Church, therefore, is a community of people who are caught up wittingly and willingly in a continuing dynamic process: that of recognizing God's saving initiative (which we call "salvation" and "grace"), and that of responding to God himself and to his work. Thus there is, as it were, a double direction to this dynamic process: that of God's coming to us and that of our cooperative response to God.

This pattern of divine initiative and human response is precisely what we discern in the person, life, and actions of Jesus of Nazareth. We acknowledge him as "true God and true man." As "true God" he is the visible outreach of God to his human family, and as "true man" he is not only the visible revelation of God but also the very paradigm or model of human responsiveness to God. This, in turn, comes to characterize the life of the Church: the same pattern of divine initiative and human response which is manifest in the life and death of Jesus becomes the pattern by which the Church lives. (Even more than that, I would add that it is the underlying pattern of all human life and history insofar as they are true to their vocation as human beings.) In the life of the Church, therefore, just as in the life of Jesus, this twofold pattern of God's initiative and our response is meant to become visible. In ordinary human life it often passes unrecognized and unacknowledged, as we overlook and fail to see the heroism of the everyday. But God has brought it to visibility in the life of Jesus, and God calls for the Church, too, to embody it from generation to generation, precisely so that people may recognize that same pattern in their own lives and commit themselves to it — to the gracious presence of God and to the recognition and obedience which that presence entails. Consequently, it is impossible to overestimate, for the well-being of the world, the importance of faith and holiness in the Church. The Church cannot regard herself as simply "having the goods" ready to hand out, as if salvation were some kind of supernatural commodity. On the contrary, she is to be a sign of redemption in a world in process of being redeemed. But the world is being redeemed from the evil which prevents it from becoming what God intends it to be, and so the Church is supposed to be a sign of hope, a sign of what can be, a promise of a better world. Even here, however, we have no room to boast, for the Church is made up of people like us; it is part of the world and is itself in continual need of God's redemptive grace and of conversion and reform in response to that grace.

THE LITURGY

In that broader context we can begin to appreciate the liturgy of the Church. The liturgy is really nothing else than the celebration of that ongoing process of redemption in and of the world. The liturgy is the "source and summit" of Christian life, as Vatican II called it, because it is in the liturgical celebration that same pattern of initiative and response, of divine action and human cooperation, which underlies all Christian life and faith, comes to its most explicit expression.

This pattern and process of divine initiative and human response finds expression in the liturgy in various ways. The pattern of God's gracious initiative, God's outreach towards us, is obviously expressed in the reading of the Word and in the gift of God's presence which comes to us through the various sacraments. But the first and basic sign of God's intervention in human affairs is the very existence of the gathered congregation. If Catholics were asked why they attend Mass on any given Sunday, most would probably say they were there because it means a lot to them, or because they like worshipping in this parish, or because as Catholics they feel obliged to be there. Yet, if we reflect on it, we have to say that the reason people gather for Mass on Sunday is that God has called them together. In contemporary society, where people believe all sorts of things or don't believe at all, the faith that draws us to church on Sunday, while one neighbor mows the lawn and another sits and reads the papers, can give us a vivid sense of vocation or calling. It is not that we are better or worse than our neighbors but that we, for God's own mysterious reasons, have been selected and called by him to acknowledge him and recognize what he is doing. The Sunday congregation, however lukewarm and listless, however confused and prejudiced it might be, is nevertheless what we refer to when we praise God on the grounds that "from age to age you gather a people to yourself."

This congregation is the sign set among the nations — or at least, set up in this neighborhood — to testify to the reality of God and to God's concern for the human race. Of course, it might not be a very good sign of God's salvation: it can be riddled with cliques, smug and self-satisfied, lacking any sense of itself as a Christian community, even rife with prejudice and soiled with social injustice. Such a community hardly deserves the name of "Christian community" at all, for to the degree its life is shaped by the ways of the world and not the ways of God it fails in its vocation to be a sign.

That is one good reason why we have liturgy and why, at the very beginning of the liturgy, we have a penitential rite. The purpose of the penitential rite at the beginning of the Mass is not so much to enable us to clean the slate of personal peccadilloes but to enable us to recognize that, although we have gathered to make visible the Body of Christ, which is the Church, we have not lived as members of that Body. We have not been faithful to our common vocation to offer to the world a sign of hope and renewal; we have not lived a lifestyle which contradicts the individualism, self-interest, and consumerism of the age; we have not shown, together, that divisions, prejudice, injustice, and indifference can be overcome through the power of God. Instead, we have developed the kind of spotty lives which enable us to merge unnoticed, like the chameleon, into our secular environment. Thus God remains unnoticed, unanswered and, indeed, helpless in the world which belongs to God but does not know God.

Still, even recognizing our common and personal infidelity, when we gather together for the celebration of the liturgy, that is what we are: a people called together by God to be witnesses and fellow-workers with God in human history. We are the Body of Christ, his arms and legs and feet and hands, for the world he loves. The liturgy, says Pope Pius XII, is the worship of the whole Body of Christ, head and members. At the liturgy, we are summoned together into the presence of the Father, who is the Father of all. We are gathered "in Christ," for without Christ we could not stand before God. And we are gathered through the Spirit of Christ, who is poured out into our hearts to form us into "one body, one spirit, in Christ."

Thus the coming together of the congregation is a sign and symbol of what God is doing and where his work is going. God's work in history, we have seen, is to gather into one the scattered children of God, to overcome divisions, to provide a place for the homeless and the lonely, to give support to those whose burdens are heavy, and to create an oasis of community in the midst of a world painfully divided into the haves and the have-nots. Here, in the congregation of God, we are all to discover our common humanity and to set aside our inequities. The gathering of believers is meant to be the anticipation of the day when God's Kingdom will be established in all its fullness, when there will be no more discrimination on the grounds of sex, race, or wealth; when there will be no more hunger and thirst, no more mistrust and mutual violence, no more competitiveness and abuse of power, for all things will be subject to Christ, and God will reign over all people in peace and for ever. In the words of Vatican II:

> The liturgy daily builds up those who are in the Church, making of them a holy temple of the Lord, a dwelling-place for God in the Spirit, to the mature measure of the fullness of Christ. At the same time it marvelously increases their power to preach Christ and thus show forth the Church, a sign lifted up among the nations . . . under which the scattered children of God may be gathered together until there is one fold and one shepherd. (*Constitution on the Sacred Liturgy* 2)

LITURGICAL CHANGES

That sounds fine in theory or as an ideal, but it was precisely to make that ideal both more credible and more realizable that Vatican II undertook the reform of the liturgy. The problem with the liturgy is that, like all enterprises involving human beings, it can get tired and stale and settle into a rut, or it can even be put to uses for which it was not intended. For example, the liturgy was from the beginning a community affair, but in the course of time it became more or less privatized. I mean not only "private Masses," but "private baptism," "private penance," and the whole way of celebrating which relied upon the activity of an authorized priest and the more or less passive presence of a congregation that was more a collection of individuals than an organic unity. As a result, the liturgy was seen as being primarily for the sanctification of individuals who were baptized, confirmed, or went to Mass for the benefit of their own interior lives. Even at Sunday Mass, the community event par excellence, people were scattered about the church engaging in their private prayers and devotions as the Mass went on at the altar.

The rubrics of the Old Mass, as they were fixed in the sixteenth century, were exclusively concerned with the priest. They began with the words: "When the priest is duly vested, he takes the chalice in his left hand . . . and carries it in front of him, his right hand resting on the burse which is placed on top of the chalice; and, making a reverence to the Cross, or to an image thereof, in the sacristy, he proceeds to the altar with his head covered and with the server going before him with the Missal and whatever else might be necessary . . ." The new equivalent of that rubric reads, "When the people have assembled, the priest and ministers proceed to the altar in the following order . . ." Moreover, the olds rubrics mentioned the congregation only three times: once to indicate the direction in which the priest should say "Dominus vobiscum;" once to suggest that, after the priest has received Communion from the chalice, "if there are some who wish to communicate," he may give Communion; and finally, to tell the priest to face the people when giving the blessing. In the *General Instruction on the Roman Missal* (1969) the Order of Mass with a Congregation is made normative, and much is made of the role of the people as a whole and of the various ministries within the assembly.

Nevertheless, if in the past the liturgy became something highly formal and individualistic, the danger today is perhaps that it often risks becoming a sort of churchy hoe-down. In reaction against the timelessness and other-worldliness of the old liturgy, and in the quest for what is often referred to as "meaningful" and "relevant," some groups turn liturgical celebrations into affirmations of life and faith which are often too flimsy and too superficial to be sustaining. Many parishes have found that the youth Masses which attracted such enthusiasm a few years ago are now becoming stereotyped and boring and that the music and lyrics collected in the now worn-out parochial anthologies have come to sound banal.

A poster in a convent chapel proclaims: "Celebrate life where you find it!" — a sentiment not untypical of the liturgies of the last twenty-five years. But the problem is, where is life found? Is this living? Faith and liturgy which are content to affirm the goodness of everything and which harp on the theme of joy, joy, joy are not true to life as we know it nor to the Christian tradition. Whereas the old liturgy tended to lock each of us into our own private devotional world, the new liturgy can be celebrated in such a way that we end up being locked into pseudo-togetherness. The painful and challenging experiences of life are simply ignored, and we pretend the Kingdom is already here or at least just waiting to be ushered in with waves and cheers.

The problem with both of these approaches to liturgy is that they collapse the tension which is inherent in Christian living and in the liturgy itself. The first, with its emphasis on the supernatural, the private, and the otherworldly, looks to a future which has nothing intrinsically to do with life on earth. Life on earth is just an obstacle course for pious souls; the Kingdom of God will be their reward in the hereafter. This view also tends to see God in heaven and the devil in the world, so that the sacraments are means of getting grace to join the one and fight the other — but all very interiorly and privately.

The other, more contemporary view emphasizes the reality of Christ's presence in the world: in sunsets and butterflies and human faces. It talks a lot about community and togetherness and love as present realities. The world is good and people are good and life is good and we are good and God is good: "Go tell everyone the news that the Kingdom is come!" Bum-bum! This view tends to see God everywhere and the devil nowhere, and the sacraments are all "celebrations," which means they ought to be fun.

TENSIONS IN CHRISTIAN LIFE AND LITURGY

Admittedly, these two views of liturgy are caricatures, and the adherents of either view could justifiably complain. I offer these caricatures, however, not so much to mock people's devotion as to call to our awareness the tension that has to be retained. And the word is tension, not balance. Tension creates energy; balance, once achieved, presumes a state of repose. No, there needs to be in our liturgy a tension between the present and the future, between the personal and the communal, between the ideal of the Kingdom and the realities of present experience in the world. In the life of Jesus, it was this tension which was the message of his preaching and work: "The Kingdom is here, in your midst; therefore repent!" (Not "have fun!") But even here where the Kingdom is, there is still a world where the Kingdom is not yet in control. We have no doubt of the outcome, but this confidence is a call to obedience and mission, not an excuse to play around. The work of God is in process: this means that we are still in need of redemption, as individuals, as communities, as nations. It means that we are not alone and that we need never despair, but it also means that we are called to work for that Kingdom, to allow God to be king, to rule in our hearts and in our society. Either to act as if all were accomplished and all were well with the world, or else to act as if the world and its affairs had nothing to do with a Kingdom that will only be established after death and out of time, would be to misunderstand both the nature of Christian life and the nature of Christian liturgy.

The liturgy is of the present, but it points to the future. It is of this world, but it points to a reality which transcends present experience. It is of the present, because it celebrates and makes real the presence among us of the God who is saving the world in Christ, but that very presence makes us painfully aware of how far we are from the Kingdom of God. It constitutes a call to live and work for the values of God, which are not the values of a society which takes for granted inequality, competitiveness, prejudice, infidelity, international tension, and unbounded consumption. The liturgy celebrates the presence of God's Kingdom, but it is a presence which contradicts us in many ways and calls us into a future that is of God's making and not a construct of Western civilization. Thus it continually challenges us to repent, to be converted, to live a new and different kind of life.

Likewise, the liturgy is of this world, yet it points to a way of being in the world which recognizes its real depth of meaning. For example, liturgy draws on all the elements of our lives: our bodies, significant persons, society, and the things we use to sustain and enhance our lives. It teaches us to use our bodies to house the presence of God, to worship and serve God, and to bring God's Word and healing to others. It teaches us to listen to the voice of God in the voice of others, and to receive at the hands of others the gifts of God. It teaches us to live in the society of others, people of different background and different race, as men and women committed to peace and unity and mutual help. It teaches us to use the goods of the earth — represented in the liturgy by bread and wine and water and oil — not as goods to be grabbed, accumulated, and consumed, but as sacraments of the Creator, to be accepted with thanksgiving, handled with reverence, and shared with generosity.

Yes the liturgy is an expression of our faith and love, but it also shapes and deepens our faith and love. It teaches us how to live with faith and how to come to deeper and truer love. It teaches us that faith, hope, and love come to life to the degree that we acknowledge and surrender to the work of God in the world. The liturgy, we know, begins and ends with the Sign of the Cross, for it is the Cross which is the sign both of God's love for us and of Jesus' human response to that love. He loved to the end, he was obedient even to death on a Cross.

Thus the liturgy brings us to the realization that there is no love without sacrifice, no life except through death to "life as we know it." In the liturgy and in life we identify ourselves with the death of Jesus, so that the life of Jesus, too, may become manifest in us. The heart of the liturgy, the heart of all the sacraments, from baptism to the rites for dying, is the paschal mystery: the mystery of God's initiative and our response as revealed in the death and resurrection of the Lord.

So we come back to where we began, to the role of the Christian community in the world. The reason why there is a community of believers is to acknowledge the work of God in human life and to cooperate with the purposes of God in human history. That work is a work of love and redemption, involving submission to God and commitment to the renewal of the face of the earth. It is not only bread and wine which are transformed in the liturgy; we are to be transformed by associating ourselves in the self-sacrifice of Jesus, that God may raise us up continually to newness of life. But it does not end there, for the bread and wine are transformed so that we might be transformed, and we are transformed so that the Church might be transformed, and the Church is to be transformed by being rebuilt under the rule of God for the well-being of all humanity.

The liturgy is not the be-all and end-all of the Christian life; Vatican II speaks of it only as the "source and summit" of Christian living, admitting that there are many other things to be done in between. Nevertheless, we can learn from the liturgy the pattern of God's presence in the world, discerning a saving Presence in all human situations in the light of God's more explicit presence in the language and symbols of the liturgy. The liturgy makes explicit what is hidden and implicit in human history: it recalls what God has done in the past, that we might recognize the same God at work in the present, and it reminds us of the goal to which the world and its history are to be directed. It puts us in touch with the mystery that lies at the very heart of things.

CONCLUSION: SOME GENERAL PRINCIPLES

This sketchy presentation of a theology of the liturgy is not going to provide easy answers for all practical questions about what must be done, whether in planning a liturgy or in living our lives. It is intended simply to serve as a basis for reflection and discussion of what we are about when we are planning and celebrating liturgies, and to offer a view of the wider context within which such planning takes place. For as we all know too well, we can get so preoccupied with the details that we lose sight of the whole and find ourselves proposing liturgical changes without much sense of the larger shape of things. In conclusion, a few general principles might be useful.

1. Liturgy is never perfect.

The liturgy we celebrate will never be adequate to the mystery it contains. More often than not, our liturgical celebrations will speak not only of the wonders of God, but of the brokenness and limitations of us who celebrate. Too easily we get caught in a critical attitude and then become angry and frustrated at the stupidity of our brothers and sisters in Christ, even to the point where we can no longer give ourselves over to the prayer of the liturgy. The only way out of that is to allow the Spirit of God to convert our indignation into compassion. This does not mean giving up the effort to improve our liturgical celebrations, but it does mean recognizing that at the heart of our liturgy stands the one who emptied himself for our sakes, the one who had compassion on the multitude, the one who was treated as a fool and put to death by those who were exasperated by him.

2. Liturgy does not always have to be different.

The temptation of all liturgy planners is to look for new and exciting ways of doing things. But liturgy is ritual, not entertainment. It is meant to form us, not have us on the edge of our seats. The liturgy keeps bringing us back to old words until we begin to understand them, and to old signs until we begin to see what they mean. Our care should be to let the words be heard, to let the images shimmer, to let the gestures be done so clearly that they speak for themselves. A corollary of this is that liturgical texts and actions should not be continually explained; they are rich in meaning, inviting insight, not explanation.

3. Liturgy is prayer.

It involves prayerful togetherness, prayerful hearing of the Word, prayerful concern for the larger world, prayerful acknowledgement of the works of God, prayerful acceptance of the gifts of God, and prayerful acceptance of the commission to go and serve the Kingdom in our lives. The place where the community gathers, wherever that may be, is not a classroom or a dance hall or a theater or a cafeteria or a private meditation room; it is a house of common prayer for the People of God.

4. Liturgy is not so much a celebration of life-as-we-know-it as it is a celebration of the mystery of life we hardly suspect.

While it uses the stuff of everyday life — word and song, movement and food, meeting and touching, candles and flowers, tables and chairs — it uses them all with a sense of the holiness of these things. This holiness is derived not so much from their presence in a sacred place as from a recognition of the sacred presence which pervades all places. The people and language and things of the liturgy are to be handled with reverence and care. Ours is a pragmatic culture, with little sense of the lovely. Part of our liturgical ministry will be to ensure that the things we use and the things we do liturgically serve to develop people's sensitivity to the loveliness of all created things, a loveliness which is but an expression and reflection of the beauty of the Creator.

5. Liturgy is "service" — an ambiguous term referring both to our service of God and to God's service of us.

Both senses of the term come together in our service of one another, for it is God who serves and is served in the mutual care we show one another. Sometimes, when we are exercising a liturgical ministry — whether it be reading or playing music or acting as an usher or a minister of Communion — we find ourselves "distracted." Maybe so. But it is also important for us to be aware of who it is we serve when we serve one another, or else our ministry itself may become distracting to others.

WORKS CITED

Segundo, Juan. The Community Called Church. *A Theology for Artisans of a New Humanity Series*, volume 1. Maryknoll: Orbis 1973.
Theisen, Jerome. *The Ultimate Church and the Promise of Salvation.* Collegeville: St. John's UP, 1976.

Chapter 2

Sacraments and Christian Living: A Reciprocal Relationship

By Michael Downey

There is an intrinsic connection between sacramental celebration and Christian living. How can we more effectively express this connection in our worship and in our daily living? Because of our human limitation and failures, this connection is not always apparent in the lives of those of us who understand ourselves, and are understood by others, as Catholics. Sacraments are often relegated to the "sacred sphere," the church building, and to specific times of the week — Sunday morning for Mass or baptism, Saturday afternoon for marriages. The rest of the week, unless interrupted by a funeral, is taken up with "worldly," or secular affairs.

The Second Vatican Council has described for us the central contours of the connection between sacraments and Christian living which will be our guide throughout these pages.

BEGINNINGS: THE SECOND VATICAN COUNCIL

For some Roman Catholics, Vatican II (1962-65) is a fading memory. Those who do remember the days of the council may recall the controversy surrounding some of the changes in Church life which originated as a result of this gathering of Church leaders. During those years, and for some time thereafter, some were startled by surface changes, like modifications in the traditional dress of religious women; some by more significant changes in the celebration of Mass, like the use of the vernacular and the new position of the alter. Others were amazed to hear of ideas such as universal call to holiness which was spelled out in the documents issued by the council.[1] The council placed before all baptized Roman Catholics, not just priests and religious, the challenge and responsibility for fully living the Christian life.

More than twenty years later, Catholics are still wrestling with the results of the council. Some look upon it as a historical mistake, and hope somehow it will go away — so that we may return to a type of Church life prevalent prior to Vatican II. On the other hand, for many, it is a matter of renewal and reform: the council is

looked upon as *the* orienting event of contemporary Church life and theology. All
Catholic life, teaching, and worship must be shaped by its spirit. By recovering a
vision of the Church as the People of God, which is based upon an understanding
of the Church in the New Testament period,[2] the council has recast our understanding of Church and Christian living so that it is closer to the Gospel and more
in keeping with the way people in the second half of the twentieth century actually
view the world, and live their lives. Those who view the council as an orienting
event do not look to a bygone era in hope that the Church may be restored to an
imagined pristine past, a pristine past which never in fact existed.[3] Rather, their
focus is on the future, on the Church as the People of God which is both servant of
and witness to the coming of the reign, or kingdom of God.[4] Central to the
preaching of Jesus, the reign of God is what God intends for the world both now
and to come. Where mercy, justice, truth, unity, and reconciliation are found, the
reign of God is near. In brief, the council attempted to raise and give partial answer
to the crucial question: What does it mean to be Catholic in the second half of the
twentieth century?

The question is crucial if we are willing to recognize that people and societies
change over time. The Church also changes. People in the twentieth century are
quite different than those in the thirteenth. Societal structures are not as they once
were. Families and communities in our own time face unique problems and
challenges. Change is a fact; whether for better or worse is another and different
question.

Those gathered at the council recognized this and set about renewing Church
life and structures so that they might better answer the urgent demands of our age.

One of the first items on the agenda was the renewal of the sacrament and
liturgical life of the Church. If the Church was to be renewed so as to meet the
pressing needs and urgent demands of the contemporary age, it was seen as
necessary, first of all, to renew that which is at the heart of Christian life.

It is clear from this that some of those gathered at the council envisioned a
reciprocal relationship between the sacraments and Christian living. Just as the
sacraments influence and shape Christian living, or at least should, so too does
Christian living shape sacramental celebration, or at least should. While most
Catholics would agree that sacraments should influence their actual Christian lives,
they do not know that their experience can be brought to bear upon the form which
sacramental celebration takes. This connection was touched upon in the Second
Vatican Council's *Constitution on the Sacred Liturgy*. In this document the liturgy
is spoken of as "fountain" and "summit" of Christian life (no. 10). The liturgy, or
sacramental worship, of the Church expresses the fullness of Christ's mystery. But
it is that mystery which leads one to worship in word and sacrament. Christ who is
present in sacrament in the reality of his death and resurrection is the one from
whom all grace flows and to whom all creation returns. The Eucharist, from this
point of view, is the ritual center of the Church's whole sacramental and liturgical
system. All other sacraments derive their meaning from their relationship to the
Eucharist and have their purpose in drawing Christians more fully into its
celebration. From this it follows that there is an intrinsic connection between the

way Christians worship and the way they live their lives. Christian living is putting into practice the consequences of belief and sacramental celebration.

NEW TESTAMENT BASIS

The reciprocal relationship between sacraments and morality, so central to the understanding of those at the council, was also a crucial concern during the New Testament period. In Romans 6 and Ephesians 5, Paul describes the practical implication of life in Christ for those who are baptized into the Body of Christ, the Church.

Romans 6 presents an understanding of baptism with particular attention to the death of Christ. Those who are baptized in Christ Jesus are incorporated into his death. Indeed, they enter into the tomb with the dead Christ. United with Christ in his death, the baptized are likewise united in the promise of his resurrection. This entails a call and a commitment to a new way of living; Ephesians 5 spells out the practical implications of this with respect to a particular way of life — that of marriage in the Lord.

In 1 Corinthians 11, Paul instructs the community that their separate groupings, divisive factions, small-mindedness, and discrimination against persons prevent them from recognizing the Body of Christ in the breaking of the bread and the sharing of the cup, the Eucharist. Those who eat and drink in the name and memory of the Lord, and do not recognize that such separations, factions, and discrimination are opposed to him in whose memory they gather and pray, bring about their own condemnation.

As in the New Testament period, the task for the Church now is one of ongoing conversion in Christ, so that what is celebrated in sacrament may be lived out by the Christian community in sight of the world. The community is central to both sacramental celebration and Christian living. They are not primarily individual or private affairs. Precisely those actions which prevent the growth and well-being of the community are condemned by Paul, and cause him to question the value and authenticity of their worship.

With emphasis upon the Church as the People of God, the Second Vatican Council likewise provided the framework for a renewed approach to both sacraments and Christian life which envisions both as rooted in the community of faith. The Church is first and foremost the People of God, a community of faith in Christ and confidence in the empowerment of the Spirit. Whatever is said of the sacraments must be said in this light. The community's struggle to live out the liberating message of Jesus in the Church and in the world, and its corporate witness to the redemptive value of the cross of Jesus Christ and to the power of his resurrection provide the basis for understanding sacramental celebration and Christian living.

THE CHANGING FACE OF WORSHIP

Because of the renewed understanding of the Church as the People of God, the community of faith in Jesus Christ and in his Spirit, sacramental life has taken a different shape than the form of worship prior to Vatican II. The history of liturgy and sacramental life is quite varied. Each epoch has worshiped differently, in a manner more or less in keeping with the Church's understanding of itself at a given period. In the thirteenth century, for example, the world — indeed the universe — was understood primarily as a rigid hierarchy of being: each and every thing was assigned its proper place and rank in the world order. The notion of a three-storied universe envisioned earth as a kind of midpoint between heaven "up there" and hell "down below." The value of beings rose on an ascending scale.

The visual imagery of higher and lower may tend to misrepresent the real benefits of the hierarchical world view of the thirteenth century. It developed in relation to a valuable philosophical view which, though it may not appeal to contemporary ways of understanding things, is admirable in its own right, and must be respected on its own terms. This view affirms that God is superior in the order of being, that higher realities influence lower realities, and that the more perfect in nature influence the less perfect. Persons, communities, and societies were understood to reflect, as well as participate in, this hierarchical order. The Church was viewed as the perfect society on earth precisely because, in its own visible hierarchy, it mirrored the proper order of things, from highest to lowest. This hierarchical ordering was understood to be ordained by God.

The sacramental life of the Church during the thirteenth century, and for many centuries following, expressed and fostered this twin understanding of the world as hierarchically ordered and of the Church as perfect image of that divinely ordained ordering. The central focus in sacramental life was the priest, whose role was to mediate between the higher realm (heavenly or sacred) and the lower realm (earthly or temporal). The priest-mediator, because of ordination, was incorporated in a unique way into the perfect, heavenly society here on earth and given power and authority to mediate between the two realms.

Whatever can rightly be argued about the advantages of this thirteenth-century view of Church and world, in the realm of sacramental life the consequences of this understanding were for the most part negative. This view of Church and world, so forcefully expressed in liturgy and sacrament, reduced the majority of Catholics to the position of observer whose role was to "assist" at Mass, to passively receive the priestly ministration of the mediator between God and humanity.

In our own day the traces of this view of world and Church are still to be found. But this understanding was set aside in favor of retrieving the biblical understanding of the Church as People of God. No longer is the Church envisioned primarily as a hierarchy, but as a community of persons baptized in grace and Spirit. It was also set aside in favor of a renewed understanding of the mission of the Church in the world, developed in the council's *Pastoral Constitution on the Church in the Modern World* (nos. 40-45). It is clearer now than before that the Church views itself in a relationship of mutuality and critical cooperation with the rest of the world. As a result, the opposition between eternal and temporal, heavenly and earthly, sacred and profane, is overcome to some degree. The Church is not only a sign to or for the world but also in the world. This is a major change in outlook.

With this understanding of the Church, what is expressed in sacramental life today is different from what was expressed in that of the thirteenth-century Church. Because it is the community of the baptized which is of primary importance in any sacramental celebration, more attention has been given to the manifold ways in which Christ is present in sacramental celebration: in the People of God who assemble for worship, in the proclamation and hearing of the word, in the various ministers of the community, as well as in the central sacramental activities of the Church such as the breaking of bread and sharing of wine, the pouring of the waters of baptism, and the anointing of the sick with blessed oil. Sacramental celebration is understood to be the act of a community of faith, not the action of one of its members done for all the rest. The central role of the community gives rise to greater participation in sacramental life. The Mass is no longer conducted in a language unfamiliar to those assembled for worship, but is celebrated in their own tongue. Responses to the various parts of the liturgy are in themselves acts of participation. The use of liturgical music more in keeping with the cultural experience of a people is likewise an indication of the participatory and communal nature of the Church's sacramental life. The altar looks a little less like a shrine and more like a table around which a community gathers to break bread and share the cup. And in the various ministries, which are more and more visible, the Church gives expression to the understanding of itself as the People of God.

In its worship and in its life the Church is a corporate witness and sign in the world. Like Paul, our attention needs to turn to the ways in which, both in sacrament and in Christian living, we are untrue to the name we bear, thus eating and drinking our own condemnation (1 Cor. 11: 17-34). The task is one of daily conversion in Christ so that what we celebrate may be lived out by the Christian community.

On the other side of the coin, however, the community's call to commitment and to conversion demands that what we are living be expressed in worship. That is to say, if we are called to ongoing conversion in Christ so as to live more fully in grace and Spirit, then sacramental celebration itself is part and parcel of that and must itself undergo conversion or change.

We must ask a few hard questions at this point. Does contemporary sacramental celebration "speak" to people in terms of what they are really living, and how they actually view things? Further, is it possible for a person to "speak" in the context of worship and sacrament what they are living, and how they view the world? Or do most of us tend to leave our true selves at home when we put on our Sunday selves and go to Mass? Does the liturgy itself express and impress a vision of God, Church, and humanity which is more in keeping with the thirteenth-century hierarchical world view or with a contemporary world view?

SACRAMENTAL CELEBRATION: SHAPED BY EXPERIENCE IN TODAY'S WORLD?

Sacramental celebration can, in principle, be shaped by contemporary events. Any view which holds that liturgy does remain unaffected by contemporary events has not taken the history of sacramental life seriously. History indicates that any view which maintains that liturgy could remain unaffected by contemporary events is naive. In our own day the Church is part of a humanity which lives in a time of such disintegration and destruction that we question whether there is any hope with which to face the future. The disorientation and hopelessness of our own age is nowhere more apparent than in the two holocausts of the twentieth century: the extermination of six million Jews and millions of others at the hands of the Nazis and the threat of nuclear war which would destroy the entire world.[5]

The two holocausts, in fact, the other possibility, remind us of the powerlessness, meaninglessness, and futurelessness which we often feel but are afraid to face. Each presents a challenge and a call to radical conversion — to a God who is with us in the midst of powerlessness and meaninglessness, and who is already ahead of us, on the other side of the fate that threatens to destroy humanity.

Sacramental celebration is a vital force in the ongoing conversion of the Christian community. But the ongoing conversion of the community does, on the other hand, demand the ongoing conversion of sacramental celebration so that it more adequately addresses the experience of persons.

What would sacramental celebration look like if the twofold holocaust were taken seriously by the Christian community at worship? To introduce prayers of petition that God grant us protection from nuclear war or that we recognize the Jews as forebears of Christian faith hardly tackles the issues of today's world — one shaped by people's experience of the meaninglessness and futurelessness signaled in the twofold holocaust. Instead, for example, more attention might be given to "lamentation" as it is found in the Bible. In homilies Christian hope must be spoken of more soberly: The days when the future of young people looked bright and promising are over. Many young people today even wonder if there will be any future for them, to say nothing of their children's future. Do preachers recognize such problems when they speak of hope and future? For many young people, it is not simply lack of faith which causes them to question the possibility of hope and future. Some have good reason to do so, and they must be addressed in this light.

In the final analysis, the hard question — however distasteful to some — is being asked by many: Can those who profess faith in Jesus Christ profess it in face of the twofold holocaust? Whatever the answer, this question must be faced.

The issue of the twofold holocaust is raised as a concrete case that illustrates some of the painful and demanding consequences of taking the connection between sacraments and Christian living seriously. Other issues and questions could be raised to illustrate the point. As a brief example, the words in Mass: "Take this all of you and eat...take this all of you and drink." Why are millions dying for want of food and drink? Because the basic necessities of life are withheld from those who need them. All do not eat, and all do not drink of the fruit of the vine and the work of the human hands.[6] Christian worship and life cannot afford to remain untouched by the events of our age.

CONTEMPORARY RENEWAL OF SACRAMENTAL LIFE AND LITURGY

What are the forms of liturgy and Christian life appropriate to our own day? Whatever answer is given, a response which is appropriate for our own age will be influenced by a renewed Christology, ecclesiology, and anthropology.[7] The way we understand Christ, the Church, and the human person has changed significantly in the latter part of the twentieth century. In addition to the pastoral and liturgical renewal promoted by Vatican II, there has been a renewal of traditional theology. Theology of the sacraments has not been untouched by this process of revision. Classical sacramental theology, the fruit of a gradual development that began in the Middle Ages, used the Christology, ecclesiology, and anthropology of that time in order to articulate its main insights. The major insights of this traditional, classical approach to the sacraments are not to be disregarded, but a renewed approach to sacramental life and Christian living needs to take seriously contemporary insights regarding Jesus Christ, the church, and the human person which have come to the fore in the life of the Church in this century.

THE RENEWAL OF CHRISTOLOGY

Christology refers to the study and understanding of the meaning and significance of Jesus Christ. Since the council, new insights regarding the meaning and significance of Jesus Christ are due in large measure to biblical research and new methods of interpreting Scripture. Strange though it may seem, one of the great contributions of contemporary Christology is the emphasis placed upon the man Jesus within the Christian mystery. In the not too distant past, preaching, Catholic teaching, and practice gave little attention to the historical person of Jesus of Nazareth. Catholicism prior to the council was, in practice, focused primarily on God's absolute otherness. One of the great accomplishments of the renewal has been the attention given to the central role of Jesus in Christianity.

A second noteworthy characteristic in many currents of contemporary Christology is the emphasis place upon the humanity of Jesus. The tradition of the Church affirms that Jesus is both truly divine and truly human in one person. Most Christians have little difficulty believing that Jesus is truly divine. The real problem seems to be that many are unable to accept or believe that Jesus is truly human. Contemporary approaches to Christology focus upon the humanity of Jesus as that which reveals the divine. This emphasis is in line with the sacramental vision of reality. First, one looks to the concrete and historical reality. Then one moves from that to what is revealed, disclosed, or signified by means of the concrete and historical reality. In the case at hand, one looks first to Jesus, the man of Nazareth, apparently like any other, and then proceeds, by means of the experience of faith, to uncover what the life, ministry, death and resurrection of Jesus mean for human beings. It is in this sense that Jesus is spoken of as the basic or primordial sacrament of God by theologian Edward Schillebeeckx in his ground-breaking work in sacramental theology.[8] It is precisely through the humanity of Jesus that his divinity and the mystery of the divine Trinity are revealed.

The recovery of the historical Jesus in Christology requires that Christian assemblies at worship remember his life and his whole ministry as this is revealed in the Scriptures and in the proclamation of the Word. In the sacramental practices of the not-to-distant past, there was a tendency to focus rather narrowly upon the sacrifice of his death in such a way that Jesus' life and ministry were not given due attention. Here the singular importance of the proclamation of the Word as a focus in sacramental celebration becomes clear. The understanding of the Eucharist as sacrifice is only properly understood if it is seen within the larger context of the story of Jesus' life and ministry. No single dimension of the Christian mystery — for example, that of sacrifice — can express the fullness of the Lord's presence. No one image, again let us say that of sacrifice, exhausts the depth of his passion. Christian liturgy is bound up with and shaped by word. The proclamation of the word, by which God's presence and action in Jesus Christ are disclosed to the assembly, serves to widen the horizon and to provide a variety of other references to the life and ministry of Jesus. Within this much broader picture his sacrifice may be more properly understood. Hence, in contemporary sacramental celebration, no one image or dimension of the Christian mystery exhausts the full meaning of, or takes priority over, the life and ministry of Jesus which is proclaimed in word and remembered in the breaking of the bread and the sharing of the cup.

THE RENEWAL OF ECCLESIOLOGY

Ecclesiology refers to the study and understanding of the Church. In this area, there have been some monumental shifts in understanding due, in large part, to some of the statements about the nature and mission of the Church which emerged as a result of Vatican II. As some of these statements have been developed by contemporary approaches to ecclesiology, the Church is less and less understood as primarily hierarchical in nature. In line with Vatican II's vision of the Church as the People of God, this view of church stresses its participatory, communal, and collegial nature. A renewed ecclesiology does not speak of the Church as the perfect society on earth. Rather, the Church is understood as a pilgrim people whose mission is to witness to the coming of God's reign and to its values: justice, mercy, unity, truth, reconciliation, and compassion, among others. From this perspective, the Church is herald and servant of the reign of God.

A second important characteristic of contemporary currents in ecclesiology makes the clear distinction between church and God's reign. From this it follows that one may not remain uncritical toward, or assign absolute value to, the ways and means by which the Church strives to bring about the reign of God. That is to say, it is the reign or kingdom of God which is of absolute value, not the Church. The role of the Church is to assist the coming of the reign, or God's intention in the world. The Church is not the reign of God. Further, the Church itself is not the ultimate judge, but itself under the judgement of the Lordship of Christ. The Church is a sign or sacrament of the reign of God. It is a concrete, historical means by which a deeper reality — the reign of God — is revealed or manifest. It is, however, not identical to the reality signified.

A third characteristic of this renewed ecclesiology, related to the second one, is its view of the Church as sign or sacrament, that is, in terms of its significance: what the Church signifies to its own members and to the broader human community. A renewed ecclesiology focuses less upon the Church as the custodian of power, truth, and holiness, and, more upon the Church as the means by which God gives concrete form to divine action on behalf of the whole human race. From this perspective the Church is that part of the human race which, in the name of all humanity, responds to God's invitation to the fullness of life.

As a result of this renewed view of the Church is the recognition of the importance of all the baptized and of their contribution and responsibility for the life and mission of the Church. It also demands that the baptized recognize their ministry to one another in such a church.

THE RENEWAL OF CHRISTIAN ANTHROPOLOGY

Anthropology refers to the study of human beings. The Christian anthropology, which has emerged from the renewal sanctioned by the Second Vatican Council, is the fruit of developments in biblical research and advanced methods of scriptural interpretation, as well as philosophical currents such as existentialism, phenomenology, and various studies in human intentionality. This renewed anthropology may be sketched in four points.

First, the human being is understood to be created in the image of God. She or he is a historical, concrete reflection of the divine, a sacrament of the life of God. This is a positive view of the human person sometimes expressed in the Church's sacramental practice prior to Vatican II. To develop and grow into the fullness of God's image, the human being must develop proper relations with God, the world, and other human beings. This positive Christian anthropology has important consequences in the sacramental life of the Church: it enables us to see the sacraments as establishing and strengthening human beings in their relationship to God, world, and others, rather than as giving grace to repair a human nature which is considered essentially depraved. This more positive view is in line with the traditional Catholic emphasis on the sanctifying, as well as healing, power of sacraments.

Second, the human person is a historical being. With a focus upon the natural and supernatural, and a very clear difference between the two, much of the world view of the Middle Ages was colored by an understanding of human nature as static and unchanging. Human nature was a "given."

The Jewish setting within which Christianity emerged was very different from this, however. Well before the time of Jesus, the people of Israel placed great emphasis on the historical dimension of the human person. A renewed Christian anthropology has recovered the singular importance of the historical. The human being is part of a history, and history is made up of relations with others in the human community. We do not exist in isolation. Our fulfillment as human beings and as Christians is never a given, never something fully accomplished. It is always something to be attained through progressive formation and ongoing participation in grace and Spirit, which come through community with others sharing a particular historical period. And history changes persons and communities.

Third, a renewed Christian anthropology views the human being as a dynamic reality. From this perspective, the person is a participant in an ongoing process of growth and change. Precisely as God's image, we are endowed with a source of energy that allows us, to a degree, to shape our lives and the life of the human community. In brief, the human person is created with a dynamism which is of divine origin and which enables the person to become more fully what she or he is, the image of God.

Fourth, a renewed anthropology sees the human person as a unity. Even to this day, many speak of the human person as a being made up of various parts. This is due, in large measure, to a dualist conception of the human person, which is rooted in Greek philosophy and which has had great impact upon Christianity. Human being, it held, consists of two parts: body and soul. In the Middle Ages, Thomas Aquinas (d. 1274) envisioned the human person as a unified being with distinct faculties of intellect, will, and sense. Some of his interpreters and some key figures in the French school of Christian spirituality of the seventeenth century did not manage to keep Aquinas' unified vision to the fore. What resulted has come to be called "faculty psychology." From this perspective the human person is viewed as having not merely distinct, but separate faculties of intellect and will.

In this view, the person thinks with the intellect and chooses through an act of the will. Contemporary views of the human person indicate that it is often not so clear cut. The end result of either the dualist approach or the perspective of faculty psychology is a vision of the human person out of keeping with the biblical tradition, where the human person is not understood as the end product of body and soul or the various faculties. Various biblical images convey an understanding of human being as a dynamic unity. The term heart, for example, describes the total unity which the person is. When used in the Bible, heart (leb and lebab in the Hebrew, and kardia in the Greek) describes the root or source of diverse personal functions. This early usage expressed the whole, total person: the person was not viewed as someone who thinks with the intellect and chooses with the will. Heart describes the person as a whole, open to attraction by others and by God. Many currents in contemporary Christian anthropology have recovered this sense of the person as a unity.

In all three areas, Christology, ecclesiology, and anthropology, dramatic shifts in understanding have occurred. It is now necessary for us to spell out some of the consequences of these contemporary insights for sacramental life and Christian living.

CONSEQUENCES OF RENEWED CHRISTOLOGY, ECCLESIOLOGY, AND ANTHROPOLOGY FOR SACRAMENTAL CELEBRATION

If the insights gained from the renewal of Christology, ecclesiology, and anthropology are taken seriously, then several consequences follow. First, our approach to sacramental life will give more attention to the Christological and ecclesiological dimensions of the sacraments. The sacraments are expressions and extensions, as it were, of Christ and the Church, or better, Christ in the Church. In a former day, the focus in the sacraments was upon the priest. But if our renewed Christology and ecclesiology are given their proper due, we come to see that the sacraments exist to give corporate and meaningful expression to Christ's presence in the Church and the Church's presence in and to Christ. The sacraments are not individual, isolated things. They are expressions of the saving presence that God is through Christ in the Church.

Second, in our approach to sacraments greater attention must be given to the human person and his or her experience. This follows from the renewal of Christian anthropology. Allowance must be made for the variety and plurality of social, cultural, and environmental elements which would naturally suggest a variety of liturgical forms. Liturgical forms, at present, do not adequately reflect actual cultural and social pluralism. Further, much is to be learned from the contributions of various sciences which are making significant gains in understanding the nature and function of symbol, the role of ritual in human life, and the various modes of celebration.

Third, the insights in each of the three areas treated help point out the intrinsic connection among the sacraments, Christ, church, and humanity. There is, as a result of renewed Christology, ecclesiology, and anthropology, a deeper awareness of the relationship between the ways in which people express their relationship of what is believed in their dealings with others in the human community. There is a reciprocal relationship between liturgy and life, sacraments and Christian morality.

APPROPRIATE SACRAMENTAL CELEBRATION

A contemporary approach to sacramental life and Christian living, informed by the changes we have considered above, requires great attention to the practical implications of what is believed and expressed in worship. In the Eucharist the Christian community expresses its belief in and commitment to the possibility of communion with God and others. It expresses the intention to work for a world in which justice will reign, and the poor and forgotten will hold first place. In the sacrament of Penance the Christian community lives out of a new vision of reality, from the perspective of God's mercy and forgiveness. Through Baptism one is invited to live a way of life based on the covenant through membership in God's people and through the power of the Spirit. This entails living according to the Spirit and not according to the flesh (Romans 8): a spirit of childhood, not of fear. The sacrament of Anointing of the Sick invites us to live in remembrance of Christ's healing ministry which provides a new perspective on suffering and death and which encourages the Christian community to care for the sick and to struggle against illness, suffering, and depersonalization.

If the practical implication of sacramental life, as briefly described above, are to be impressed upon the Christian community, then appropriate sacramental celebration is required, not simply desired. Liturgical celebration must give expression to the renewed Christology, ecclesiology, and anthropology which we have treated.

Sacramental celebration appropriate to our age takes seriously the truth that the Church is the People of God, sacrament of Christ in the world. Before all else, the Church is the community of the baptized. Whatever is said of ministry in the Church, ordained or nonordained, must be said in this light. This understanding of the Church might be called laical (from the Greek laos, "people"). This perspective focuses upon persons in community who are the Body of Christ. The keynotes of this understanding of church are the categories of People of God, communion, prophecy, and service, not hierarchy, power or authority.

Appropriate celebration of the sacraments today would give a great deal of attention to the formative role of the Word. Since the Second Vatican Council, increasing attention has been given to the place of the Word in liturgy. In the period just prior to the council, the Scriptures did not have a prominent place in the lives of many Roman Catholics. When used in liturgical settings, the Word was often used improperly. In contemporary liturgical practice, the proclamation and the hearing of the Word are looked upon as manifestations and disclosures of the presence of God. It is in the Scriptures that the community learns the story of Jesus' life and ministry. Appropriate sacramental practice requires that due attention be given to the Word as formative of Christian life. As a result, planning and preparation for proclamation, hearing, and preaching must be kept to the fore as singularly important values. In the hearing and proclamation of the Word, the community receives and expresses its identity as the Body of Christ, as it does in the breaking of the bread and sharing of the cup, or in the anointing with oil or chrism.

It should be clear from what has been suggested above that the primary symbol in any sacramental celebration is the gathered assembly. The singularly important role of the assembly is described in detail in the Constitution on the Sacred Liturgy of the Second Vatican Council (nos. 7, 11, 14, 27).

To take but one example, music should be selected with the assembly in mind. It is to be chosen on the basis of its ability to lift the assembly's mind and heart to God, not simply because it sounds nice or is easily sung. In practice music is sometimes selected because "everyone knows this one," thus requiring little by way of preparation or planning. Music which sounds good may or may not invite the community to participation. Here one must raise the question: Is liturgical music an act of ministry, or service, which invites prayer and worship of a community, or is it simply a good performance for the pleasure of the congregation? Environment calls the assembly to worship. Music creates environment.

In these days since Vatican II, there has been a tendency to confuse good sacramental celebration with good liturgical music. But good liturgical music is not the same as good sacramental celebration. Strange as it may seem, liturgy requires far more planning, preparation, and know-how by all involved than does first-rate liturgical music. Ordained and nonordained, all liturgical ministry is done from within the assembly and for the assembly. This means that priests and other liturgical ministers must consider themselves, first of all, as baptized Christians, part of the community that God calls.

From this it follows that the ministry of the presbyter (priest) in presiding at liturgy is a ministry to the assembly. Likewise, all other ministries. It is on this base, an apostolic (which implies being sent to) and sacramental base, that the sacrament of Holy Orders rests. Even if one would insist on an essential difference between the priesthood of the ordained and the priesthood of all the baptized, the point remains that the task of all who serve as ministers in the Church's liturgy is to serve or minister to the assembly.

This kind of thinking demands a breadth of liturgical ministries. It means that there must be a change of mind regarding the role of the assembly. Without this there is no true sacramental celebration and no effective communication of the practical implications of the sacraments for daily Christian living, only those who say Mass and those who attend Mass. Everything, even preaching, has to be affected by this change of mind.

If the primary focus in sacramental celebration is the assembly, then several consequences follow. First, the more people involved in a liturgical service, the more important the coordination of the various ministries. This is the role or job of the presider, or priest. Second, liturgical ministry demands adequate preparation. Third, to preside at liturgy means to have a comprehensive understanding of what is taking place. This cannot be done without touching bases with all the liturgical ministries involved. This is best done by entering into the liturgical planning process.

If it is true, as has been suggested in this chapter, that the sacraments themselves express a Christian view of human life and of the world, and if this is to be communicated to those who celebrate the sacraments, then allowance must be made for a variety of liturgical forms which better enable the Christian community to express and receive its identity as the Body of Christ in today's world.

END NOTES

[1] Walter M. Abbott, editor, *The Documents of Vatican II* (New York: America P, 1966). All references to the documents of Vatican II are based upon this edition. Hereafter, references to the documents, as well as to Sacred Scripture, will be included in the text. All scriptural references are from the Jerusalem Bible.

[2] The significance of the notion developed in the council's *Dogmatic Constitution on the Church*, chap. 2, is ably explored by Sandra M. Schneiders, "Evangelical Equality," *Spirituality Today* 38, no. 4, (Winter 1986): 293-302.

[3] For an excellent analysis of the way in which the period of Christian origins is sometimes imagined as a "golden age," see Robert L. Wilken, *The Myth of Christian Beginnings* (Garden City, NY: Doubleday, 1971) 18ff.

[4] The term reign of God is preferable to kingdom of God for several reasons. Among these, the term reign better expresses the active nature of God's intentional coming to be in the world. The term kingdom often carries the connotation of place and space, as if God's kingdom were a sort of cosmic playground or glorified geographical location.

[5] This theme has been treated at length in Michael Downey, "Worship Between the Holocausts," *Theology Today* 43, no.1 (April 1986): 75-87. The issue is also treated in John Pawlikowski, "Worship after the Holocaust: An Ethician's Reflections," *Worship* 58, no.4 (July 1984): 315-29.

[6] For a fuller treatment of this point, see Monika Hellwig, *The Eucharist and the Hunger of the World* (New York: Paulist , 1976).

[7] On this point, I am indebted to the insights of Raymond Vaillancourt, *Toward a Renewal of Sacramental Theology* (Collegeville: Liturgical , 1979).

[8] Edward Schillebeeckx, *Christ the Sacrament of the Encounter with God* (New York: Sheed & Ward, 1963).

Chapter 3

Worship: A High Risk Invitation

by Walter Brueggemann

One's interpretive, hermeneutical assumptions about worship make a great deal
of difference. We all have such interpretive, hermeneutical assumptions, even if
they are not articulated or intentionally arrived at. Such assumptions come partly
from our theological tradition and partly from our perception of the context in
which we worship. In turn, our perception of the context of worship is shaped, in
part, by our socio-economic-political setting and interests.

NO GIVEN WORLDS, ONLY CONTRIVED ONES

The thesis I wish to explore is this: Christian worship is based on the evangelical
conviction that the world in which we live is *not a given but a contrivance*. It will be
clear in what follows that I intend this as a dramatic, not an ontological statement. I
believe that our social reality is essentially dramatic in the sense that it is arrived at by
the free play of interaction and a series of decisions that could have been made
differently from the way they have been made. Thus I use the word dramatic
intentionally, seriously, and realistically, to speak of a world that we have chosen and
constructed over a long period of playing parts through the process of our life.

The great temptation in the jeopardized Western world at the end of the
twentieth century with its presuppositions that are primarily white, male, and
imperial, is to imagine that the world as we know it and value it is a set, fixed,
closed, absolute world. That world has been the way it is so long, and it is mostly
the way we like it. In our cultural innocence and lack of social awareness, we may
judge the world to have always been so, and to assign to it an absolute legitimacy.

That temptation is clearly as wrong as it is seductive. We may state that
wrongness in three dimensions:

1. Berger and Luckmann have helped us *sociologically* with the programmatic
phrase "the social construction of reality."[1] It is my judgment that worship cannot
be critically understood at all without access to this social concept. The phrase

asserts that *the world of power and meaning is largely achieved and fabricated through the administration, management, and manipulation of social symbols.* That administration is done intentionally in a community in order to arrange power and value in certain ways, aimed at creating a viable social sphere in which to live. Every community, from family to nation-state is engaged in such world construction in "liturgical activities" that range from family activities — such as table prayers and birthday celebrations — to national events — such as press conferences, political conventions, and sports extravaganzas. The world of "free market economics," or "one man, one vote," or "no shoes, no shirt, no service," is made by the management of symbols which could have been managed in other ways. Over a period of time, the manipulation of symbols begins to create values, perceptions, and patterns of behavior.

2. Schafer, Fowler, and Kegan, along with a number of other *psychological* developmental theorists now urge that human personality is not a fixed structure but is an ongoing process in which the subject person is an active agent in the formation of self.[2] That is, the self is not a given imposed from the outside, even though powerful forces act to impose, but the self is a network and carrier of self-selecting choices. The person as self with a strong ego center is a process of dynamic development, still under way. No doubt factors of heredity and environment are present, but finally *the voice of the person as volitional agent is decisive.* This of course leaves open the theoretical possibility that this volitional agent should have acted differently and a very different self could have emerged.

3. *Theologically*, a biblical understanding of God's creature, that is, of God's creative work, makes clear that "creation" is not a one-time happening "at the beginning," but is a process through which *God continues to form and shape creation as God wills it.* Thus Gen. 1:1 is very likely to be translated, "When God began to create..." which means that God is still at work and we creatures are not yet finished. That is why we sing with Charles Wesley:

Finish, then, thy new creation; Pure and spotless let us be;
Let us see Thy great salvation Perfectly restored in Thee;
Changed from glory into glory, Till in heaven we take our place,
Till we cast our crowns before Thee, Lost in wonder, love, and praise.

God's work of creation is not yet completed. The world is still being formed (see 1 John 3:2).

On all three counts, sociological, psychological, and theological, we reject the temptation to take the world as fixed, closed and settled.

EVERY COMMUNITY IS SHAPED
BY SELECTED SLOGANS, POEMS, AND STORIES

This construction of world, of social reality, of personal identity, is not a technical, mechanistic process. It is rather a poetic, artistic, dramatic enterprise that depends upon the mediation of symbols through which we receive, appropriate, select, and discern our life experience in certain ways.

1. World-making, society-making, person-making is primarily a process of imagination, that is, the use, articulation, and reception of certain images and figures as true voices of reality.[3] We are imaging, imagined, image-processing creatures in the image of God. We are not flat, one-dimensional biological creations. We are evoked in certain directions by words spoken over us, commandments issued us, promises made to us, images placed ahead of us.

We know about the formation of self-concept through the long practice of various metaphors, for example, "good boy," "naughty girl," "high achiever," "trouble-maker," "discipline problem," as powerful forces which shape reality. As that capacity to shape reality is true of personality formation, it is equally true of the formation of a community which is susceptible to the shaping of ideology and propaganda. Communities may be taught and persuaded to fear, to hate, to be inferior or superior, to accept oppression as God-given fate. Managers of public symbols can create confidence in the economy, can mobilize support for war, can generate acts of compassion by the management of public imagination. That is what the power of the media and the advertising industry is all about.[4]

2. While imagination is an act of immediacy, authoritative imagination is not of the moment. It is based in stories and poems (often reduced to slogans) in which the community has come most to trust. As we become more aware of our sexism and racism, we begin to notice how selective and prejudiced is much of our tradition of treasured narratives. Nonetheless present imaginative acts are funded by a memory which the community regards as normative, that is, canonical. The narratives may be those of ancient Israel (Exodus, Sinai, David), of Jesus (parables of the kingdom, stories of miracles, narratives of resurrection), of the family ("the day we first met," "the first day of school," "the day the baby came home"), of the church ("when Pastor X came," "when we had the choral program" "when we burned the mortgage"), of the nation (the landing of the Pilgrims, the Gettysburg address, remember Pearl Harbor, the betrayal at Munich). These narratives which have been carefully selected and carefully stylized, begin to shape a world and legitimate certain language, certain epistemology, certain perceptions, certain behavior responses which are judged appropriate. Eventually they become sanctions for policy.

3. The practice of imagination and the function of a canon of identity-giving narratives yields certain governing metaphors for the community. These may be constrictive metaphors that shrivel life, energizing metaphors that give life power, or bold metaphors that authorize, control, and dominate. As Berger and Luckmann have shown, the utilization of imagination, narrative, and metaphor leads to the proposal of a world that is first objectified as real, and then internalized as mine.

Every community over time develops patterns of presentation (liturgies) whereby it transmits and mediates its chosen set of images, narratives, and metaphors in authoritative ways to form a certain world for its members and adherents. Such a world is experienced as true, reliable, legitimate, and worthy of adherence. It finally is embraced as mine.

Our first two points together insist a) that the world in which we live is contrived and not a given, b) that contrivance is done through liturgy which administers memory in ways that mediate and make available a certain world. The liturgic enterprise wants to make that world so clear, reliable, and binding that is received as an ordained given. But it is not. There are no given worlds. And therefore the liturgic processing is urgent and must be done regularly and with intentionality. If the world-creating liturgy is not done regularly and with intentionality, that world may lose its credibility. Its adherents may fall away when it is noticed that it is a contrivance. One can argue that social revolutions of slaves in Egypt to become Israel, of peasants in Nicaragua, of women against sexist orderings of society, happen when people begin to notice that the world is not given but only contrived. They withdraw allegiance and refuse any longer to participate in or give sanction to the contrivance.[5] They no longer practice approved behavior, conformity, or cooperation. Then the world has a chance to change, but such change is perceived by those who value the old world as disintegration.

OUR CONTRIVED WAY OF LIFE

The dominant contrived world for American Christians is wrought through powerful intentional liturgies of which we are mostly unaware. But the fact that we are unaware does not keep us from regarding this contrived world as real and objective, nor from internalizing it as mine.

1. The notion of personhood that is mediated to us through the liturgies of dominant culture, that is, through TV commercials, is that *we are formed and shaped to be consumers.* Our world is presented to us as filled with commodities (products) which overcome every problem, every headache, every loneliness. We are imagined to be satisfied, satiated consumers. Moreover, we are portrayed as isolated consumers who enjoy private satiation, so that even in the contrived conviviality modeled in TV commercials, no one ever speaks meaningfully to anyone. The satiation and gratification are presented as immediate and complete. There are no hopes that reach into my future, nor into the future of the next generation, nor any such hopes that reach out beyond self toward community. Satiation and well-being are very narrowly expressed in terms of both time and space.

2. The social world mediated to us by dominant cultural values is fundamentally *a world of economic success and well-being* in which affluence in the midst of competition is how the world is said to be organized. Thus the public image of success in competition coheres with the personal image of satiation through commodities.

3. The created order of international affairs is portrayed generally *as a divided world set into armed camps* in which our capacity for economic well-being and success, as well as our chance for personal satiation through commodities ("maintain our standard of living") must be guarded. The economic monopoly we enjoy must be maintained. Those who challenge that economic monopoly are dismissed as terrorists or revolutionaries.

The end result of this constructed world, wrought not out of reality but out of administration of imagination, is a world of fear and insecurity which breeds anxiety, defensiveness, and despair which is often acted out as brutality and inhumaneness.

I shall not take time here to argue the point, but I shall, for the purposes of our discussion, offer an assessment of this world wrought through imagination:

1. *It is clearly contrived, not an objective given. The goals of life in terms of success through competition and satiation through commodities are not givens in the world.*
2. *This world is a lie because it is not in touch with the root experiences of human persons which concern human hurt and human possibility, which are screened out in this portrayal.*
3. *This constructed world theologically is an idolatrous contrivance, because it offers a perception of reality organized against or without the reality of God's rule, with the reality of judgment or the power of grace.*

Insofar as a Christian congregation participates in this contrived world, as we all inevitably do, that congregation will be fearful, weary, ill-focused, and lacking in energy and courage for serious obedience to the gospel. The congregation awaits renewal because it lives in a world which militates against newness. Newness derived from the gospel subverts this contrived world.

OFFERING AN ALTERNATIVE WORLDVIEW THROUGH LITURGY

It is the task and opportunity of the Church's liturgy to liberate people from this contrived, false, idolatrous construct of reality which robs us not only of faith, but of humanness. In order to do that liberation, the liturgy of the Church must offer an alternative construct of the world which is mediated through different narratives and metaphors, which provides and legitimates an alternative imagination, and which offers alternative pictures of the world. In our cultural context, the Church's liturgy is characteristically counter-liturgy which subverts the presumed world acted out in the dominant liturgies. The Church does its subversive work not by ethical admonition and heavy-handed coercion but by making available an alternative construction of reality which legitimates and makes possible a life more faithful, more obedient, and more joyous. Thus I do not suggest that a liturgy must be innovative, up-beat, or experimental in the standard usage of those words, as much as it needs to be honest, intentional, and nervy about the practice of reality that is done in this liturgy.

I suggest four theological themes which are pertinent to and subversive for American Christians who are enmeshed in the dominant false construct. Others might be added, but these seem especially obvious and urgent.

ADMIT OUR PAIN, RAGE, AND GRIEF

1. Human persons and human community live always with the *reality of pain, rage, and grief* which need not be denied as our culture wants us to do, but may be precisely a medium of communication with God.[6] Our culture wants us to deny and cover up the pain. Very many people have the impression that it is "meet, right and our bounded duty" to pretend that life does not hurt. That is correlated to a false notion of God who does not traffic in grief, rage, and pain.

I submit that the liturgical tradition is overly preoccupied with guilt when in fact honesty about the world leads to a recognition that there is more pain, rage, and grief in the world that has been generated by our guilt. Moreover, if the church were to recover, for example, the psalms of protest and complaint, we would see that these social realities of pain, rage, and grief are proper material for conversation with God. We know experientially that there will be no moving on with our life until these transactions with God bring our social reality to speech. In a society of cover-up and denial, the liturgic practice of honesty can permit new vitality in the community and in communion with God. Said another way, worship must face the fact that the large issue of theodicy remains unresolved and must one more time be carried to the throne of God.

ARTICULATE GOD'S RULE

2. *The rule of God* in the world is not simply a traditional formula nor a pious affirmation, but is a reality of life that guards us against anxiety and despair. The rule of God, of course, is a cliche for church people, but most of our liturgy is not serious enough or dangerous enough to see that the celebration of God's sovereignty or the Lordship of Jesus Christ is, in fact, a polemical statement with immediate practical implications.[7] To sing the Doxology or Gloria Patria is, in fact, an act of dethroning and delegitimating other would-be claimants of our loyalty.

The sneaking suspicion we mostly have is either that no one rules and I am on my desperate own, or some power rules that wills me no ultimate good. If no one rules and I am on my desperate own, I am hopelessly fated to anxiety. Because of my occasional honesty, I know that I am not adequate to maintain my life, to sustain my social role. And so I live in a frenzy of being fast or smart or tough enough to pretend (to myself) that I am adequate. But it is a lie. Or if some power rules that wills me no ultimate good, I am lost in despair because that power which may be a norm of financial success, or a fantasy of sexual adequacy, or my job, or my economic goals, whatever it is, it leaves me hopeless because I can never measure up. And that awesome power which is never satisfied, will never be defeated or displaced in my life. The biblical word for these pretenses that lead either to anxiety or despair is idolatry. Liturgy which liberates joins issues with those idols around the articulation of God's rule.

The liturgy of the Church summons us away from those idols and asserts the truth of God's governance as a rule of one who is weighty in judgment and massive in grace, who is more for us than we are for ourselves. Every time Israel said liturgically, "Praise Yahweh," it is said under its breath, "and not Baal." Every time Israel said, "Who is like Yahweh," it knew the answer is "Nobody, not any of the petty gods who eat at our life." Every time the early Church confessed, "Jesus is Lord," it understood that Caesar had been dethroned and delegitimated.

Christian congregations that are exhausted by fear and intimidated by insatiably demanding gods, have little energy and cannot notice beyond themselves. The liturgy is the place where the true governance of God is enacted and dramatized. But it does no good unless, in that liturgical moment, it is clear that for an instant the destructive idols have lost their power and we are free of their endless demands.[8] For this imaginative moment, the nagging stops, the quotas cease. For a moment we have freedom to be who we are called to be, opportunity to be present with the one God who is a proper, legitimate authority of grace and truth in our life. As the defensiveness yields, we find ourselves for a moment able to be generous, able to get our mind off self long enough to care for others.

RECOGNIZE OUR UNION WITH NEIGHBORS

3. Other people in the world are not just inconveniences or burdens, but *they are God-given brothers and sisters* in this journey of life. They are conversation partners, sources of life and hope without which we cannot live. The point is so obvious. But it is also intensely difficult in our society committed to gross individualism and so covetous of greedy isolation. Here, more that anywhere, the Christian liturgy may join issue with the lies which have become a virtue in our capitalist, free enterprise system.

Solidarity with sisters and brothers belongs to the Church's celebration of creation. It is incongruous that the very voices of creationism (vs. "evolutionism") are also the voices which promote the destructive heresy of individualism. Clearly God's creative activity is aimed at the formation of a human community. The gift of creation is enacted in Israel by the making of covenant and the summoning of persons into community. Covenant partnership among human persons cuts across every line of demarcation that the world wants to establish. The Bible knows that the world's delineation of strong and weak, rich and poor, haves and have-nots is dysfunctional in serious communities of trust, praise and obedience (Gal. 3:28).

The liturgy evokes a world that permits us to move out of our pathological isolation. It is not intended that we should be alone either in the world or before God. It is precisely engagement with brother and sister which the Bible identifies as resurrection to new life (1 John 3:14).

As the congregation begins to envision a world of human solidarity, strange, powerful things happen. We do not need to hoard, guard, or protect our energy or our goods, because we learn that such goods and energy multiply when made available to the community.

REAFFIRM THAT GOD KEEPS PROMISES

4. Christian liturgy enacts the claim that *God's promises* while not yet kept, are still underway and are coming to fruition. God has promised a world of joy, peace, freedom, justice, and well-being. That is a very different promise from the ones made by our world which concern private comfort and disproportionate well-being.

The promissory character of the Gospel asserts that the world is not closed, because the creation is not finished. Most of us are trapped in a technical reason which believes that the possibilities are all now available, and there is nothing left to do but to move the pieces around. We so believe the myths of scarcity that we accept a zero-sum theological verdict on the world.

The narratives of miracle preserved in our tradition counter that atheistic claim. God's world is freighted with gifts we have not yet received. Some of these narratives are in the Bible, such as the manna story, the feeding and healing miracles. But some of these stories are present, visible, and powerful in the life of the contemporary community as we stop to notice when strange healings occur. The liturgy is the enactment, most visible in the Eucharist, that God gives gifts for life in the face of tired selfishness which believes there are no more gifts yet to be given.

I suggest that on all four points, the Church joins issue with the lie fashioned by the world of fear. Each such event of truth-telling permits a transformed community to emerge:

1. *Against the cover-up, the reality of pain, rage, and grief when in conversation with God becomes a source of vitality, because God joins us in our hurt.*
2. *Against the despair and anxiety or no governance of false governance, the rule of God who is advocate for us permits us to leave off our paralysis and fatigue, and begin to notice the world out beyond us.*
3. *Against our isolation, the liturgy makes visible brothers and sisters who are gifts from God who mediated life to us, which rescues us from our fearful isolation.*
4. *Against the fearful closure of technical reason, the liturgy dramatizes the openness of the world for the gifts of God which God has yet to give and the impossibilities that God will yet do.*

ALLOWING CORPORATE WORSHIP
TO TRANSFORM THE REALITY WE LIVE

These and related assertions out of the Gospel over a period of time begin to yield a counter-world in which we can live differently.

1. *We begin to perceive self not as a passive consumer who establishes worth not by having things, but as a child of God bound to brothers and sister under God's unutterable benevolence.*
2. *We begin to perceive that the community is not a collection of threats and competitions, but includes those who will suffer with us and rejoice with us (1 Cor. 12:26).*
3. *We begin to perceive that the world is not a fearfilled armed camp, but is the place where God's governance makes new life possible.*

What begins to emerge is a community of people who perceive the world differently and who can therefore act differently, in trust and obedience. I am aware that these suggestions do not cohere easily with classical models of liturgy, but sufficient correlation can be made to legitimate this perspective. I am, in any case, convinced that worship which renews in a way that lasts, will not happen by new style or by new technique, but only by a decision that this community regularly acts on a reality different from the one the world perpetrates on us. There are a variety of strategies which may be utilized, but finally the fact of subversive countering of culture will need to be faced.

I am aware that this is a high risk invitation because the world is so much with us. But insofar as we have courage for evangelical reality, such a liturgical imagination of an alternative world will indeed renew the Church.[9] That renewal is not measured first of all by the response of the world. What counts first is a community with freedom and courage to live free from the lies of the world for the sake of the world. Clearly the liturgic conventions provide place for such enactment. But what is required is theological intentionality and the courage to imagine a world different from the projections of Pharaoh and Caesar. Such a liturgic act requires a liberated imagination which in turn requires disengagement from the hopes and fears of Pharaoh. Rescue by God from slavery has always required departure from the empire and its quotas. The insistence of good liturgy is always, "Let my people go." But this is followed by the sovereign claim, "That they may serve me."

END NOTES

[1] Peter L. Berger and Thomas Luckmann, *The Social Construction of Reality* (Garden City: Doubleday, 1966). See also Peter L. Berger, *The Sacred Canopy* (Garden City: Doubleday, 1967).

[2] Roy Schafer, *Language and Insight* (New Haven: Yale UP, 1978), James W. Fowler, *Becoming Adult, Becoming Christian* (New York: Harper, 1984), and especially Robert Kegan, *The Evolving Self* (Cambridge: Harvard UP, 1982).

[3] On "people-making" in another sense, see Virginia Satir, *People Making* (Palo Alto: Science and Behavior Books, 1971).

[4] See J.F. Kavanaugh, *Following Christ in a Consumer Society* (Maryknoll: Orbis, 1981).

[5] Following George Mendenhall, Norman K. Gottwald, *The Tribes of Yahweh* (Maryknoll: Orbis, 1979): 326, 408, has understood "withdrawal" as the decisive act in the formation of the biblical community.

[6] See Walter Brueggemann, "A Shape for Old Testament Theology, II: Embrace of Pain," *Catholic Biblical Quarterly* 47 (1985): 395-415.

[7] Robert Martin-Achard, "A Propos de la Theologie de l'Ancien Testament," TZ 35 (1979): 63-71, has shown how doxological worship and theology are characteristically polemical.

[8] On God and the idols see Pablo Richard et al., *The Idols of Death and the God of Life* (Maryknoll: Orbis, 1983). This collection makes clear that the real problem of modernity is not atheism but idolatry.

[9] The urging made here for worship is resonate with suggestions about education made by Jack L. Seymour, Robert T. O'Gorman, and Charles L. Foster, *The Church in the Education of the Public* (Nashville: Abingdon, 1984) 135-56.

Chapter 4

Improving Worship for Youth

By Thomas N. Tomaszek

Standing apart
I heard you say hello
it was sweet of you to try
but I was (after all)
standing apart.
Nancy Nelson, 17 (Strommen 21)

Whether we speak in psychological or physical terms, youth often stand apart from our worshipping communities. That troubles us. We know that many youth do not go to church. We have been told that many of those who do attend liturgy find little meaning in the ritual. We assume that some of youth's separation, in mind or body, from the rest of the community is attributable to the stages of adolescence (that is, by experimentally defining who I am not, I begin to understand who I am.). We also know that whether or not youth attend church is often an irritant in family relationships. In whatever terms we choose to describe this situation which concerns parents, youth ministers, pastors, parishioners and youth themselves, it's hard to deny that problems exist.

There are aspects of this dilemma which are related to the general condition of parish life, a discussion of which is not my intention here. Issues such as the need for adult catechesis and parenting programs, continuing formation for homilists, presiders and liturgy teams, and related concerns have a direct impact on the meaningful experience of worship for all age groups. I will try to identify the specific issues and problems which may cause youth to feel alienated from our worshipping assemblies, and then begin to explore some practical actions we can take as communities to change the situation.[1]

Let's begin by trying to understand how all liturgy has an impact on our lives. Can you remember a particularly meaningful Eucharistic liturgy in which you've participated? Take a moment to recall some of the specific images that you may still remember. Were you with friends, family? Was it a special occasion such as a wedding, Confirmation, or perhaps after the death of a loved one? Were there special circumstances such as on a retreat, with a group of close friends, or held in a special environment such as outdoors or in someone's home?

After you've remembered as much of the physical details as you can, try to recall how you felt during and after that liturgy. How would you describe your feelings? spirit-filled? energized? challenged? uplifted? Did the experience bring about a feeling of reverence for God's presence in your life? a motivation to change? a sense of community with those present?

My presumption is that the people you were with and their actions toward you and toward each other were a major reason why you felt the way you did and why you remember that particular liturgy. Those memories and the experience of community are alive in you and have become part of the faith you bring to each liturgical celebration, just as I imagine that early Christians gathered to remember and celebrate the presence of Jesus in their midst.

Recognizing that our faith grew through the people we encountered is probably not surprising; we often experience God through the people who touch our lives. In *Music in Catholic Worship*, the liturgy is referred to in this language of relationships. "People in love make signs of love, not only to express their love but also to deepen it. Love never expressed dies. Christians' love for Christ and for one another and Christians' faith in Christ and in one another must be expressed in the signs and symbols of celebration or they will die." *(Music in Catholic Worship* 4)

"DO THIS IN MEMORY OF ME:" THE FOUR MOVEMENTS OF LOVE

In any love relationship, the interaction of the lover and the beloved flows in a distinct pattern, or series of movements. The first movement is one of choosing—to select or choose, to be moved toward one another. Secondly, after the initial expressions of love, there is a desire to give to the other person, either through actions or gifts, as a way of demonstrating that love to one another. Thirdly, love calls for a change of heart, a certain transformation of identity as the lovers are re-oriented from consideration of self-need to an inclusion of the well-being of the beloved. Finally, the bond of love moves lovers toward a common future as gift to others.

The movements of love are more cyclical than linear in time, as various events may change the nature of a relationship. For example, a husband and wife who have recently experienced a painful separation after infidelity, or profound joy after the birth of a child, may find themselves acting out the beginning stages of courtship as a re-establishment of the relationship. Similar recommitments also occur in other types of relationships besides a marriage. Each movement within the cycle deepens the relationship and strengthens the bond between lover and beloved.

The relationship at the core of our liturgical action finds its origin in the covenant made by Yahweh with the people of Israel. The dynamics of that covenant are observable throughout the Old Testament in the lives of Abraham,

Moses, David, and the prophets. Jesus' words for those covenantal movements of love are Take, Bless, Break, and Give. To illustrate, we read in Genesis how Abram was called by Yahweh and taken from his homeland; given the name Abraham, blessed with the promise and then reality of children and a new homeland; broken repeatedly, first by leaving his homeland, later by the challenge to sacrifice his son Isaac; and finally, given to the people of God as the father of many nations—symbol of God's faithfulness and love.

Jesus is the fulfillment of that covenant begun with Abraham and testified to by the prophets. The movements of love observable in salvation history are also identifiable in Jesus' life. First, Jesus is chosen simply by being the Son of God. Scripture gives evidence of this relationship in the words of the Father as Jesus is baptized by John: "This is my beloved Son in whom I am well pleased." He is blessed by the Father's trust and gift of the apostles and disciples, and finally, all of humanity. Through his suffering and death He is broken; and finally, by his resurrection He is given so that the human family might become a gift to the Father.

As members of Christ's body, we are called to believe that each of us, as individuals, but, more importantly, as community members, has been chosen by God to give witness to that covenant. We believe that in every event of our lives we have been blessed or gifted. Such is our understanding of grace. We are called to be broken, to be transformed from lives of self-centered values to a relationship as world family, so that we, too, may become gift to others and to the Creator.

We commemorate, in the Eucharist, Jesus' life, death and resurrection, and we commit ourselves to that covenant of love as God's chosen people. Our Eucharistic prayer reflects this anamnesis: Jesus took the bread, blessed it, broke it, and gave it to his disciples saying, "Take this, all of you, and eat it, this is my body which will be given up for you." If we are to be given for the life of the world, then we also must be transformed —transubstantiated— as we believe the simple of gifts of bread and wine to be. To live is to love in family. Not to do so is to die.[2]

I believe that these four movements of love also hold the key to understanding the difficulties which many young people have with the expression of covenant relationship we call the liturgy. The dynamics of these movements provide us a framework from which to discern, first, the problems implicit in adolescents' experience of liturgy, and then, the community's action necessary to improve the worship experience for its young people. For as youth gain experiences of liturgy as the communal action of which we spoke earlier, they will be pre-disposed and better prepared to assume leadership roles within our faith communities.

PROBLEM #1: OUR LITURGIES DON'T ATTEND TO YOUTH

The first movement of love, **Take**, is a movement towards one another. The initial stages of any relationship are marked by a paying attention to the other, a singling out and calling of one another in such a way that the loved one knows of our feelings. In a wedding ceremony the bride and groom take each other as husband and wife. In baptism, we are claimed for Christ by the faith of the community. In Jesus' own life, both Simeon and John the Baptist give witness to the One claimed for a singular role. Likewise, a ministry to youth is first characterized by its outreach, calling forth, and paying attention to the needs of young people.

Liturgy is about relationships. More specifically, liturgy is an expression of our relationship within the body of Christ and with God. When Jesus asked his disciples to "do this in memory of me," he was calling for our commitment to a long-term relationship with the other members of that body as a response in faith to God's love. Our faith allows us to believe that Jesus is still with us and present as we gather to share the Word and break bread. The disciples on the road to Emmaus finally recognized the Lord in the breaking of the bread. Likewise, our liturgical action calls us to recognize and celebrate our communion with one another as the body of Christ.

There are a variety of levels by which we are personally present to one another at the Sunday Eucharist. Besides our commitment in faith, our response is also conditioned by our culture which requires us daily to participate in rituals with little or no personal meaning. Take, for example, the cultural ritual of shaking hands when meeting a person for the first time versus a handshake between long-time friends greeting one another after a prolonged absence. There's an obvious difference in the level of personal investment or commitment which characterizes each of those symbolic greetings (rituals).

Still another example might be our intention in asking someone, "How are you?," as a part of polite conversation, as contrasted with a mother phoning a child away at college to ask, "How are you?" In the first case, the intention of the questioner is usually no more than a public form of greeting. It reveals little about the relationship involved. Would we consider stopping our routine at that point to really find out how the person is doing? Yet, the same ritual question by the mother to the child is likely to lead to an intended sharing of the stories of life on campus.

Both these examples might serve to illustrate the role that commitment and intention have in creating an atmosphere of mutual concern among members of the worshipping assembly on Sundays. My premise is that much of the uneasiness which we sometimes feel about our liturgies arises from an implicit sense that our worship time needs to bring people together in both a physical and soulful way. When that doesn't happen, when the liturgy is not meaningful for us, for whatever reasons, we begin to look for ways to inspire it with meaning, or we abandon it, either by becoming apathetic or by leaving.

I liken this instinct to how we approach any relationship we may have which is not going well. At first, our intuition tells us that things are not right. We may talk about our feelings with the person(s) involved. We may even seek professional help in sorting out our feelings. We look for ways to improve the relationship. If our efforts fail, or if after repeated attempts the other person ignores our efforts, we may leave the relationship just to save our own sense of self-esteem.

PAYING ATTENTION TO THE NEEDS OF YOUTH

Defining self through developing relationships is one of the cornerstone tasks of adolescence. Especially for younger adolescents, "who I am" is often understandable only by observing "who I'm with." For youth who are struggling with an awakening sense of self, in addition to other adolescent crises, remaining present while being ignored in church may be too much to confront. Parents and adults may call for youth to look beyond the immediate experience, yet such a task may be developmentally impossible.

Charles Shelton argues that, "Although a relationship with Jesus Christ may be of major importance to the adolescent, the larger, more impersonal settings that characterize traditional religious practice often distract the adolescent and actually militate against his or her developmental need for more personal, relational forms of worship. The adolescent suffers a lack of meaning from these impersonal forms of worship that, in turn, reinforces a growing sense of alienation from the church." (Shelton 144)

In a world filled with empty rituals and broken or strained relationships, I believe all people, young and old alike, are looking for honest and meaningful relationships. More directly, the idealism of adolescence has little tolerance for hypocrisy. Regis Duffy points out that, "The argument of the young person is, often enough, one of honest ritual: why go to Mass 'just to be there?' Such an argument begs the real question: how much connection must there be between our stories and our intention before our rituals are honest?" (Duffy 90)

I do not believe that we ever outgrow our need for personal, relational forms of worship. But it has been my experience that most of the parish weekend liturgies which I have attended are not very personal. The time spent together does not seem to help the people gathered to relate to one another. Throughout my own adolescence and especially in the last few years when I have been on the road frequently and in need of worshipping with other communities, besides a quick handshake at the sign of peace, I have not experienced a feeling of welcome or a sense that anyone knew or cared that I was there. I do not believe I was ignored, merely a victim of the benign neglect characteristic of the rite as we have come to experience it. And I know that I have been equally guilty of not welcoming new people in my home parish.

The intention of welcoming, by definition, ought to require attention to each other, a movement towards one another as we give praise and thanks to God. It doesn't seem that we understand what it means to be the body of Christ. At least, I do not think we have figured out how to translate our understanding into the practical ways of relating to our neighbors during worship. That is an issue we will have to address if we want youth to feel less alienated and attend our communities' celebrations.

Improving worship for young people will come from attention to not only the particulars of the worship experience, but also attentiveness to their stories and to their developmental needs. Such attention must be shown within the context of worship as well as through other appropriate experiences of personal faith sharing with significant adults in their lives. Parents' roles are not to be under-valued for this most basic element of catechesis. We have to believe that the other relational opportunities our parishes and parents provide—from scouting, sports and other social programs to the time that parents spend with their children—all serve to lay a foundation upon which the worship experiences may be faith-filled expressions on the part of youth.

Moreover, the whole community shares in the responsibility to share its story with the young. This is one of the foundational principles of effective youth ministry. *(Vision of Youth Ministry* 9-10) "That is why 'liturgy' cannot be viewed solely in terms of 'ceremonies.' It must be the vehicle of values, it must convey meaning; this implies diversification of the liturgy according to cultural milieu as well as fidelity in expressing the foundational actions that have been handed down in the tradition." (Dalmais 234)

Thomas Groome describes such faith-sharing as having multiple dimensions: believing, trusting, and doing. "When the Christian community assembles to offer common worship, it is symbolizing and gathering together there an offering of lives of Christian 'praxis.' Conversely, there flows from that liturgical activity a renewed commitment to live lives of Christian service. Thus liturgy is both an expression and a source of Christian faith in all three of its activities." (Groome 65)

The connection between life and liturgy will be taken up in greater depth later. Yet, as we attempt to understand the absence of youth from active participation in our parishes a certain amount of pragmatism is necessary. Regis Duffy notes, "If, during the preceding week, our familial and professional lives have permitted us to be only minimally aware of and responsive to our own and others' presence, there is no theological reason for supposing that this situation will suddenly change in church." (Duffy 85)

SUMMARY

Liturgy is, first of all, a movement towards one another. Liturgy is an expression of the faith community's relationship with God and with one another. As adolescents, youth find difficulty in relating to the larger, more impersonal liturgical practices which seem to be the norm in many parishes. To improve worship for youth, parents and adults need to consider ways through which youth are attended to more personally at liturgy, and ways in which the community attends to youth needs through other outreach ministries.

PROBLEM #2: OUR YOUTH DON'T ATTEND LITURGY

The second movement of love, **Bless**, is characterized by the exchange of gifts—either objects or actions—which become signs of love and fidelity. At a wedding the couple exchange rings as a sign of their love and fidelity to one another. In confirmation, we celebrate the gifts of the Holy Spirit. During Jesus' public ministry he performed miracles—giving sight to the blind, curing the lepers, raising Lazarus—as signs of his oneness with God. We are blessed by the gifts we receive. Likewise, a ministry to youth affirms and celebrates the gifts and talents that young people bring to the community.

In reality, most of the exchanging about liturgy which takes place between adults and youth is usually argumentative, and often results in a misplaced emphasis on youth "going to church." It is somewhat of a Catch-22 for parents. Liturgies do not attend to youth; youth do not attend liturgy. Seldom asked is the larger question about what is more important to adolescent faith development.

In his article, "Can the Liturgy Speak to Today's Teenagers," Michael Warren theorizes that liturgy is "expressive human activity" which, in a Christian sense, is "an action by which a community expresses its attitude about (the relationship) between this group and the Spirit of Jesus." (Warren 225) Through liturgical action we remember and celebrate what we believe.

Unfortunately, for many of us, the expression of that faith relationship (liturgy), too often becomes the whole relationship. To put it another way, instead of liturgy manifesting how we live out our Christian commitment and values from day to day, we may pay more attention to how we express those values as a group. "Going to church" becomes more important than "being" church, being Christ for one another. *(Constitution 9)*

It is my conviction that we pay too much attention to how youth express their faith instead of nurturing and affirming the faith that already exists in their lives. We worry about whether or not adolescents attend Sunday Eucharist instead of providing more opportunities for them to experience the Christian life in action. I say this not to diminish the importance of encouraging anyone, especially young people, from participating in the liturgical action of the community, but rather to emphasize the need to assist youth in developing their relationships with God. Good relationships will seek expression. Good liturgies will express the depth of those relationships. *(Music 6)*

While liturgy is often, unfortunately, the battle ground between parent and child, the underlying need for a welcoming community and new models of responding to contemporary youth concerns is really at the heart of the solution. Improvements can be made in liturgical practice, but those changes won't bring more youth to church on a regular basis unless supported by a comprehensive outreach of caring opportunities for young people.

BARRIERS TO AFFIRMING THE FAITH OF YOUNG PEOPLE

One of the most consistent barriers to affirming the gifts which young people have to contribute to the Church is parents and church leaders' inability to overcome their fears about adolescents. Youth are not adults. They act differently, talk differently, dress differently and play differently. It is their right to be adolescents, which means they also have the right to make mistakes and to be not as sure of themselves as adults might be. Adults who find themselves in the position of advocating for the needs of adolescents would do well to educate the community on the developmental tasks of this age group.

One of those characteristics is the tendency to come to faith through trial and error; the "via negativa" of defining self and belief through deciding what not to believe in. Dr. John Nelson points out that, "To integrate personal integrity and corporate identity is particularly difficult for adolescents, because they have to push things apart before they can pull them back together." (Nelson 11ff) In a sense, adolescents, developmentally, are non-believers who become socialized into the faith community.

Simply telling youth that liturgy is important is not likely to convince them to attend Sunday worship. They want to know why liturgy is important. They need to know why others think it is important. Good experiences of liturgy in other settings or with peer groups will begin to provide those answers. Regular contact with caring adults of the parish in other programs will also help. Opportunities to participate in the preparation of liturgy and in the liturgical ministries will enable youth to witness to other youth. Sharing time as a family (or in a peer group) before or after attending Eucharist together will also lead young people to value liturgy.

Another systemic factor in determining whether youth will attend worship regularly, is the faith praxis of their parents. "Without excusing young people from their responsibility to search for the faith, we must also be responsible for the credibility of our celebrations of faith in the eyes of the young. Flawed Christians are not a stumbling block to these young people, but uncommitted Christians are." (Duffy 42)

Youth ministers and other church leaders face an uphill struggle in developing the faith of adolescents whose parents infrequently attend Sunday liturgy, or who have minimal ties to the faith community. It is not uncommon for a young person to have a peak faith experience on a retreat or through a small group liturgy, only to find little common ground to share that experience with a parent. Improving worship for youth will occur most successfully when part of a long-range plan of developing Christian formation experiences for all age groups of the parish.

THE NEED FOR AUTHENTIC SYMBOLS

Turning our attention to the worship experience itself, we may need to examine the authenticity of our liturgical symbols for clues in explaining why youth do not attend Sunday Eucharist. "The diversity of people present at a parish liturgy gives rise to a further problem. Can the same parish liturgy be an authentic expression for a grade school girl, her college-age brother, their married sister with her young family, their parents and grandparents?" *(Music* 17) *Music in Catholic Worship* also goes on to suggest that special celebrations for smaller, homogeneous groups may be one alternative to dealing with the diversity of expression appropriate for such a range of ages present in the assembly.

Theologically, the liturgical assembly is symbol of our unity in the Body of Christ, which through Christ, and by the power of the Holy Spirit, gives witness to God in action and presence. In pastoral practice, that symbol loses some of its authenticity when the meaning of the rite is obscure to many of those assembled, particularly the young. The liturgy involves a form and structure which acts as a symbol, that is, the expression of the relationship also symbolizes the relationship. We have a need to ask then, if our symbols represent the relationship accurately. As Joseph Gelineau points out in *The Liturgy Today and Tomorrow*, "With symbolic signs, in ritual as in art, form and content are inseparable. The medium is also the message." (Gelineau 16)

It might be argued that authentic symbols cause what they signify (the theological principle ex opere operando), and that a well-celebrated Eucharist implies that all members have entered into the expression. I would argue for more opportunities for youth to experience Eucharist and other forms of liturgy in the company of their peers, thereby encouraging an adaptation of the rites to achieve their participation and understanding.

There are many practical implications of scheduling peer-group Eucharistic liturgies, including the limited availability of clergy, but it is my sense that such experiences will only serve to enhance the parish celebrations through the increased participation by youth. Scheduling other types of communal worship is an approach youth ministers and parish liturgist should consider with equal weight. Overlooked are creative celebrations of morning and evening prayer, communal reconciliation services and other devotional prayer experiences. The rhythms of the school calendar also lend themselves to ritual celebrations (for example, welcoming younger adolescents into the group each fall, a "homecoming" celebration at the parish for those who have been away, a special blessing prayer for the evening before semester exams, connecting "spring break" with Lenten prayer, or a graduation celebration in spring.)

We may still need to address the difficulties which all members of the assembly often have with the liturgical praxis in our local communities, but through the experience of creative peer-group liturgies we will have instilled in young people a hunger for the spiritual nourishment which is the summit of our Christian heritage.

SUMMARY

In the movements of love, we recognize our responsibility to love youth as Jesus loves—unconditionally—and to affirm their faith at whatever depth or circumstance their belief may be. Though they leave our communities to test that faith, just as the prodigal son chose to leave his father's house, so we must welcome them back with open arms and rejoicing, as the father set a feast for his son's return. Parents and adults will demonstrate this openness by focusing on young people's developmental issues and needs; by allowing youth to mature in faith at their own pace; and by providing peer-group liturgical experiences and other Christian leadership development opportunities for youth.

PROBLEM #3: OUR LITURGIES DON'T SPEAK TO THE SIGNS OF THE TIMES

The third movement of love, **Break**, implies change, adaptation and the challenge to grow. It recognizes that the beginning of a new life together is an acceptance of death, at least in the sense of moving beyond what exists now, to what can be in the future. In marriage, the two individuals become one family—a process which requires a willingness to adapt an individual lifestyle to the needs of the other. The *Mass of Christian Burial* emphasizes the change which is necessary to enter into eternal life. Jesus' own death broke the bond of sin, thus his suffering achieved a new life for us. And in ministering to youth, especially those broken by the pressures of our society, we challenge them to grow in faith and confidence in using their talents and gifts for the good of the community.

The image of Jesus breaking the bread at the Last Supper is a powerful one. As the story has been handed down to us in the Christian scriptures and through the art of many centuries, the scene creates an engaging visual which is easily recalled within the symbol of Eucharist as a shared meal.

Less immediately engaging is the symbol of Jesus' life being broken for us. Jesus was a change agent who, by his life and ministry, challenged the commonly held perceptions about society, the law, and traditional values. Measured by the standards of his culture, his life ended in failure—crucified by the authorities, abandoned by his friends and disciples, and ridiculed and rejected by the leaders of his church.

We believe that by Jesus' entering into the brokenness of our humanity, we have been united to his resurrection. His life was the instrument of our salvation. (*Constitution* 5) Yet, our current liturgical practice seems to indicate that we still have trouble connecting the two symbols of broken lives and broken bread. Let me illustrate.

FROM LIFE TO LITURGY

The following story appeared on the Associated Press wire service the Sunday following an incident in which an African-American man died after being chased by white youth in Queens, New York:

> "Shouts of 'Go Home,' 'Resign' and 'You have no right to be here' met Mayor Edward Koch as he arrived Sunday at Our Lady of Grace Roman Catholic Church in Howard Beach, Queens." (12/28/86)

Following the death, there had been considerable racial unrest in the area, with marches and demonstrations reminiscent of the civil rights movement of the 60's. The mayor had visited the church in an effort to calm tensions in the neighborhood, pleading for racial harmony.

As I remember reading that account, I was curious to know how the other members of that assembly reacted to the behavior of the shouters. Was it just a few hotheads? How did the presider respond? Did everyone just ignore the situation and get on with the ritual? Did the mayor respond? Ironically, or maybe appropriately, the readings for that Sunday were from Paul, "Bear with one another; forgive whatever grievances you have against one another." (Col 3:14), and from Matthew's account of the flight into Egypt. I wondered what the homily was about and, finally, how the shouters felt at the end of that liturgy. Or did they stay for communion?

While the incident is now history, I believe it illustrates the psychological distance which we often create between our worship and the everyday events of our lives—the signs of the times. We have developed an attitude toward liturgy that neither expects it to challenge our assumptions about current social and inter-personal issues, nor expects us to respond to the implicit challenge of the liturgy's symbolic action. We have become spectators at an event which calls for us, through our presence, to be co-actors. (*Constitution* 14)

For youth who are accustomed to sitting through presentations, lectures and non-participative classroom situations, the format of the liturgy must often appear to be just another time to sit patiently, listen, and to not respond unless called upon. Challenging such images will require challenging ourselves. David Power suggests, "It is the engagement with life that we need to bring to worship, the readiness to be challenged to self-understanding by an affirmation of the holy that gives perspective to the appropriation of new social and inner experience. (Power 290)

Part of that self-understanding will come from recalling Jesus' life as one which confronted the ideologies of his day, and by addressing what needs to be confronted in our own life and culture. Part of our understanding will also come from the challenge to gather at liturgy to share our "brokenness" with one another so that we might rejoice in God's saving action in our lives. Not to be overlooked is the power of prayer as an intercessory action. Liturgy challenges us to evangelize ourselves and our culture.

Had I been there in Queens that day, I would have wanted some time to reflect on the terrible events which had taken place that week in my community. I would have wanted to "break open the Word" to understand how the Gospel was calling us to respond to those events. I would have wanted to talk about contemporary flights into Egypt which happen everyday from Nicaragua, South Africa, modern Israel, as well as Howard Beach.

I hope those people had that opportunity, but my guess is that they dealt "abstractly" with the need for patience and peace. I would have been frustrated. Mike Warren speaks to this need to integrate liturgy and life when he states:

> Liturgy is expressive human activity, a symbolic expression of the life of a particular group of people. It does not speak to, it speaks from. It does for the life of a group what sharing a meal does for married couples. Eating together embodies more than personal nourishment; it embodies a way of being together. In the same way, the liturgy is more than personal devotion. It is the assembly's way of life. (Warren 85)

We need to find room within our liturgies for this sharing, this "being-together" to take place. We need opportunities to meld the complementary symbols of the shared meal and the call to radical change. But first we will need to confront the societal and cultural issues involved, including our own attitude about how much time Sunday worship should take. If Sunday's (or Saturday evenings) were a time which we each set aside for reflection and renewal in the context of community, we might gain the necessary insights to creatively confront the contemporary issues and personal needs. We might even have an opportunity to collectively take action on pressing concerns.

One vision for this time is an expanded sense of the Gathering Rite—a time for people to talk with one another, when youth might be gathered on their own for awhile and then return to worship with the adult assembly. *(Directory for Masses with Children* 17) It will be our common prayer together, about our hopes and dreams, our struggles and failures which will unite us in worship—not in the abstract, but in the language of our everyday lives.

GATHERING FOR EACH OTHER

Our usual response to this lack of significant relating which occurs in our worship, is to consider quick-fix solutions. "If only Father related better to youth...If only the choir director would use more upbeat music...If only the older

people wouldn't sit in the back of church...If only we had better homilies... If only
the ushers really greeted people as they came in..." and so on. Usually the
comment refers to what they could do.

We all have our lists, and without much doubt, there are numerous practices
which could significantly improve the quality of our worship. But such attention to
the form and style of liturgy diverts our attention from far more serious issues.
Mike Warren notes, "We are in danger of trivializing our liturgical and catechetical
concerns. There is a lingering possibility that liturgists may become pre-occupied
with the worship act or event and forget that its context is the life of a group of
persons who do or do not embody Gospel values in deeds, not just in words."
(Warren 86)

It would be wrong to presume that liturgists, homilists, or presiders are solely
responsible for such a complex problem without understanding our own role. At
the heart of the issue is our own presence and sense of the sacrament.[3] Here again,
our culture conditions what we expect to take place at worship.

We have an insatiable appetite for entertainment—from spectator sports, to
movies, videos, concerts, television and even "people-watching" at the mall.
Youth, in particular, have been conditioned since infancy to be visually entertained.
Is it any wonder to us that we have the same desire to be entertained at liturgy by
hearing a good homily or by listening to songs we enjoy? This is not a vote for
boring homilies or uninspired music, but rather, an appeal to not let our cultural
predilection for entertainment undermine our responsibility to be involved in the
liturgical action.

The major question remains: Do we take liturgy seriously? Do we mean what
we pray? Do we say what we mean? Do we understand the evocative power of the
symbol as we gather together in Christ's name? As Ralph Keifer suggests, "Jesus'
command was 'Do this,' not 'Say these words.'" (Keifer 102)

Faced with contradictions in deed from the speech/liturgy of our assemblies,
and guided by more idealistic, less jaded images of the world, some young people
may choose not to align themselves with our communities. Charles Shelton
comments: "A key question that adolescents frequently ask is, 'If I believe in
Jesus, why do I need the Church?' This question often results from the adolescent's
experience of dull liturgies or the human limitations of church leaders, or the
failure of Catholics to personally live the Gospel." (Shelton 152)

Through the movements of love, we will need to continue challenging young
people to be the leaven of change within our communities, and to make the
community's prayer their own. Youth who have become disenchanted with life and
liturgy will need our care, understanding and supportive challenges to move
beyond their hurt or despair. Youth who have left will need to know our
commitment to embrace them with open arms as they return. That is our challenge
as youth advocates: to preach the Good News in word and deed.

SUMMARY

Liturgy does not exhaust the activity of the Church, but rather, is its high point.
Members of the assembly, by virtue of their baptism, have a right and

responsibility to take an active part in the liturgical celebration and to allow liturgy to shape and express their lives of Christian service. Young people become easily disenchanted when liturgy is a non-authentic symbol of Christian commitment. Through attention to how we gather at Eucharist, and to how we involve youth in the mission of our faith communities, we will begin to lay the foundation for improving young people's worship experience.

PROBLEM #4: WE NEED LITURGICAL FORMATION

The final movement of love, **Give**, is characterized by action which prepares the loved ones to go forth into the community united in spirit and deed. To give a gift implies a preparation of what is given as well as a willingness to give. The wedding ceremony exhorts the newly married couple to be witnesses of God's love and to be open to the gift of children. Candidates for the sacraments of initiation are prepared through catechetical experiences. Jesus prepared for his ministry through fasting and prayer. A ministry to youth, by continually affirming their unique talents and gifts, seeks to prepare young people for leadership in the faith community.

Because we stand as those in the world who bless the Lord, we have come to see the vital importance of being prepared to stand in the sanctuary of blessing that the liturgy is; any other approach is deemed criminal in the halls of kingdom justice. (Fleming 111)

The implicit challenge of Austin Fleming's statement above is to create a catechesis for liturgy which responds to the developmental needs of both youth and adults. Previously in this paper, we have seen how current liturgical praxis may need to adapt to fully allow for youth participation. But the task of preparing for liturgy should be an ongoing catechetical goal for all members of the assembly, young and old alike.

The radical liturgical reforms promulgated by the Second Vatican Council, which restored liturgy to its essential role as an action of the entire Church, have not been met with equally creative (if not, radical) methods for catechizing the faithful to assume responsibility for their liturgical action. Adults, as well as youth, need to understand more about what happens and is supposed to happen when we gather for Eucharist. Most importantly, there is a need for us to see our role as actors rather than audience. Participation and presence take on new meaning when we fully understand our part, and that "because it acts sacramentally, a community becomes a sacrament—an enduring sign of grace in...human affairs." (Whitehead 46)

At issue is our understanding of catechesis. If we limit ourselves to the "classroom" notion of Christian formation we may have experienced as youth ourselves, we may never consider the broader intention of catechesis: formation of the total person. (NCD 39, 185) This formation could occur in a variety of ways, but initially should help people make the connection between liturgy and the other rituals in their lives. Weddings, anniversaries, births, and holidays all call to mind important touchstones of human interaction. Through understanding the roles that these types of events and relationships have in our lives, we will be better able to grow toward a new awareness of our role in the Eucharistic ritual.[4]

DEVELOPING A CATECHESIS FOR LITURGY

We are catechized through liturgy, that is, the experience of worship also serves to teach us about worship. This is why positive experiences gained through peer-group liturgies may be extremely valuable in "teaching" young people about the meaning of worship in a Christian's life, as well as their role in the community's worship.

Gilbert Ostdiek, OFM, suggests that we also need catechesis for liturgy to prepare people to participate. He makes several contrasts which are helpful here.

> Unlike catechesis through liturgy, this second form of catechesis focuses directly on the liturgy itself. But it is not just rehearsal or training in how to do the liturgy, nor is it a form of theological reflection done in abstraction from the actual celebration, like sacramental catechesis of the past. Rather, it is a reflection on the liturgical rites which seeks to break them open to the understanding of the participants. (Ostdiek 10)

He goes on to point out that catechesis for liturgy needs to account for the diversity of our assemblies, both in age and faith maturity (to which I would add cultural disposition or heritage), and therefore be available in every phase of life. In keeping with sound developmental learning principles, liturgical catechesis will aim to help all worshippers learn from their own experience. Finally, liturgical catechesis should take into consideration the richness of symbols and symbolic action as a way of communicating about ourselves as whole persons—minds and bodies (a point not lost on those of us who have worked with junior-high aged youth).

Developing a sound catechesis for liturgy may be no small task. As I have alluded to earlier, one of the weaknesses of our current liturgical practice is our lack of attention to many of those present in our assemblies. The tendency to ignore certain groups of people is due more to our own oversight than it is a conscious attempt to exclude, but it is no less alienating to all cultures, particularly youth. It may also be symptomatic of problems in the whole of our society. Regardless, we need to develop a sense of "appropriate" liturgical expression which allows music, gesture, preaching and art to be from other than the dominant culture.

Too often our response to this diversity is to homogenize the faithful, allowing only for adult forms of expression. Youth who most regularly attend church, do so because liturgy gives them a sense of belonging. (Strommen 100) When we exclude youth and other minority cultures from active liturgical participation, for whatever reason, we risk alienating them from the community. More significantly, the emergence of Hispanic, African-American, Native American, Asian-American and other non-European cultural traditions has provided us with an opportunity to learn about and share the richness of all cultural expressions of faith and worship. *(Constitution* 37)

My own experiences as a liturgist for large gatherings of youth have demonstrated to me the catechetical effect of integrating a multicultural emphasis on liturgical expression. Song, dance, ritual gesture, cultural symbols and dramatization can heighten the liturgical experience for all ages present. The more recent availability of hymnals for African-American and Hispanic Catholics and the culturally-oriented liturgies celebrated for youth and Native-American Catholics during the visits by Pope John Paul II in the United States have had a positive impact on our awareness for the cultural adaptation of liturgy.

YOUTH CATECHESIS FOR LITURGY

Liturgical catechesis for youth begins when adults of the community are willing to listen to and respond to young people's faith experiences. Instead of being challenged by young people's difficulties with going to a weekend liturgy and appealing to the law, we, as adults, need to offer youth deeper explanations of the personal reasons or motives which have brought us to our faith and Christian commitment. Charles Shelton suggests several important themes to keep in mind when ministering to adolescent questions about religious practice: conveying our own sense of faith commitment and the importance of Eucharist in our own life; and, assisting youth in understanding where they find strength and support for their values, especially if Eucharist is not a priority in their lives. (Shelton 159)

There are a number of immediate steps we can take to improve worship for young people. In the workshops I have given on this topic, frequently the response of the adults who attend is that the situation is beyond their control and in the hands of those who plan or preside over the liturgy. Not to argue with their feeling of helplessness, I suggest that they keep in mind three overall strategies:

1. First, an effective approach to any problem-solving is to begin with the aspects of the problem which you can control. Any positive action will change the overall situation and may then lead to other positive steps which can be taken later. The point is that something can be done, even if it is not what you ultimately would hope to accomplish.

2. Secondly, a problem is rarely solved by only one intervening action. You will need to be committed to a long-term effort which may involve several or many intermediate steps. I like to think of it as a "stepular" approach to problem-solving.

3. Do not confuse liturgical problems with people problems. Many of the difficulties we face in improving worship for youth have less to do with the form and content of liturgy and more to do with the people involved. You will need to know about both, which means becoming knowledgeable about liturgy, but also, getting in touch with your best sense of improving relationships with the people responsible for planning or preparing liturgy.

Finally, I suggest that continued dissatisfaction with liturgical practice is at least a healthy sign that renewal is possible. The alternative is apathy and rejection which is a far more complex issue to address.

TWO MODELS FOR ACHIEVING YOUTH PARTICIPATION

It should be evident by now that there are two paths for achieving greater participation by young people in the community's liturgy. The first is through attention to their presence in the assembly and adaptation of the community's celebration to include their forms of expression. The majority of the suggestions which follow in this article address this concern for involving youth in the parish liturgy and liturgical ministries.

The second model is by providing creative Eucharistic and non-Eucharistic liturgical experiences for youth in peer groups. These may occur in parishes, through collaborative efforts by several area parishes, within Catholic high schools, on retreats, or through leadership training events, to name a few possibilities. As described earlier, such opportunities allow youth to grasp the meaning of liturgy as communal action in ways which better relate to their culture, disposition and faith development. (Other chapters of this volume will address creative suggestions for youth liturgies.)

SUMMARY

Preparing for liturgy is a right and duty of all Christians. At issue is our understanding of the role of catechesis in this preparation. We are catechized through liturgy, and we recognize the need to catechize for liturgy by attention to lifelong developmental Christian formation. We assist the catechetical process by familiarizing ourselves with other cultural expressions of worship—including an understanding that youth have a unique cultural identity. We begin to improve worship for youth by sharing our own value for Eucharist in our lives, by involving them regularly in parish celebrations, and by providing small group and peer group celebrations.

My own premise is that paying attention to our collective understandings and best instincts about relationships can help us begin to improve worship for all of us, especially youth. Take, bless, break, then give. As we are reminded in Deuteronomy 30: 11,14: "This command is not too mysterious and remote...it is already in your hearts; you have only to carry it out."

SUGGESTIONS FOR IMPROVING WORSHIP FOR YOUTH

I have divided some specific suggestions into four categories: the need for experiences of community, the need for peer group liturgies, the need for advocacy, and the need for liturgical formation.

SUGGESTIONS FOR PROVIDING EXPERIENCES OF COMMUNITY

1. Encourage youth to attend weekend liturgy together. (They may have to agree to an every other week rotation to allow for family time.) Announce which service you'll be attending and ask youth to join you for breakfast (or supper) afterwards. If this is not possible, meet in the lobby or church hall before or after a weekend liturgy for casual talk.

2. Offer to convene a special liturgy planning committee of youth who will prepare a parish "back-to-school" liturgy in the fall, a liturgy for the feast of Holy Family in winter, a graduation liturgy in the spring and a vacation blessing liturgy in summer. That's at least four times a year that youth will have contact with the parish.

3. Have the youth group sponsor a coffee/juice and donut Sunday once a month, or once a season (maybe after those special liturgies as above). Use it as a publicity event for announcing other projects or youth events. Have each youth invite another friend who does not regularly attend weekend liturgy.

4. Above all, begin to understand that all community building opportunities for youth will help them to feel more a part of the worshipping assembly. This means regularly scheduling activities and events which counterprogram the variety of opportunities available to youth through school activities, and other organizations.

SUGGESTIONS FOR YOUTH LITURGIES

5. Schedule special youth Eucharistic liturgies, prayer services or communal reconciliations periodically. Involve youth in the planning of these times so that the liturgies reflect their preferences in music, prayer styles, storytelling and environment. One suggested pattern is mentioned in #2 above. Another effective approach is to collaborate with other area parishes or the Catholic high school. High school and campus ministers would most likely have a good sense of youth liturgy and homiletics. (These events are most effective if they happen on a regular basis.)

6. Schedule a Word Service for youth a half hour before the most attended Sunday liturgy. (Perhaps a young adult would take responsibility for this session, or would coordinate youth in rotating the preparation.) Include listening time to contemporary Christian music or other reflection music, storytelling and time to share about the week's events. (The idea is that you may not be able to change the parish liturgy, but you can provide a meaningful worship time for youth each week which leads them to participate in the community prayer.)

SUGGESTIONS FOR ADVOCACY

7. Appoint or designate one adult (more if needed) to act as an advocate or lobbyist for the needs of youth within your worship community. This person should maintain a close working relationship with two or more youth from your community, thereby enabling the young people to speak on their own behalf, and to ensure a realistic perspective of youth needs, not just adult expectations.

8. Advocate for two youth to be chosen as voting/active members of any liturgy planning committees, especially those for special feasts such as Christmas and the Easter Triduum. Have these youth give regular reports back to the other youth for comments and suggestions.

9. Lobby the presiders and homilists to use at least one example in the homily or prayers each week which will relate directly to the lives of young people. Propose your willingness to supply such examples from a group of youth if they'd be used regularly.

10. Survey youth to find out which songs from the hymnal or missalette they particularly like, and which songs they consider boring. Involve the liturgist or choir director in your plan, or if this is not possible, diplomatically present the results later on. Make sure two or three articulate youth are present at that meeting to help explain some of the choices. The purpose here is to show that certain songs are more likely to gain a response, rather than to only point out the negative received songs. (Note: this meeting may require some pre-lobbying on your part.)

11. Be a talent scout for youth who are good singers, instrumentalists, or artists. Link them with those who are responsible for planning liturgies and environment, or music in your community. (A good source of information might be high school art or music teachers.)

12. Seek youth who can assist in planning the church environment for the seasons. Artists and other artisans—in-training should be encouraged to use their gifts.

SUGGESTIONS FOR LITURGICAL FORMATION

13. Establish an apprenticeship program for youth involvement in the liturgical ministries (Greeters, Lectors, Eucharistic Ministers). In this model, a youth advocate pairs adolescents with adults who agree to act as "mentors." For example, an established lector might work with a young person on technique, then split the readings at her next scheduled responsibility.

14. Integrate a capsule curriculum on liturgy and the sacraments into the regular youth discussion time. Smaller doses of theory can be combined with experiences of various prayer forms. Focus on relationships and communication.

15. Offer specific liturgical and skill training for young singers, cantors, instrumentalists, and liturgy planners that include music reading sessions, skills building, input on the liturgical ministries and opportunities to prepare liturgies for their peers.

16. Spend time discussing the current season of the Church year. Share stories about family customs and rituals which are observed. This is also a good way to reflect on rich cultural traditions which can be included in worship.

17. Schedule opportunities to experience the worship of other cultural groups. Experiences of Native American, Hispanic, Asian or African spiritualities can open understandings of the diversity of our faith tradition and prayer styles.

18. Form Bible study or informal discussion groups to read the upcoming readings from the Lectionary. (This should be done on a regular basis to be effective.) Have group members take turns summarizing the discussions and offer the results to the regular homilists. Ask them to include parts of the discussions in their homilies.

19. Use the same procedure of reflection, discussion and presentation for sets of general intercessions, or prayers of thanksgiving. (Make sure the homilists or liturgists are aware of the process you use so that results will be taken credibly.)

END NOTES

[1] I wish to note here that I frequently use the term liturgy to describe the experience and rites of Eucharistic liturgy, though the word itself can be used to describe a variety of worship experiences. Communal celebrations of morning or evening prayer, reconciliation, benediction, and other devotional prayer can all rightfully be understood as liturgy. In fact, such liturgical experiences can aid adolescent participation in the Eucharist.

[2] I am indebted for this concept of love's movements to the Rev. Joseph Kremer and his presentation at the National Association of Pastoral Musicians' Regional Convention, at Collegeville MN, in June 1980.

[3] I have found Regis Duffy's sacramental theology in Real Presence (San Francisco: Harper And Row, 1982) to be particularly insightful.

[4] For a concise theology of worship, see Eugene Walsh, Gathering For Each Other (Nashville; Pastoral Arts Associates, 1981) and Mark Searle, Liturgy Made Simple (Collegeville: Liturgical Press, 1981) for basic liturgical principles.

WORKS CITED

Constitution on The Sacred Liturgy. The Liturgy Documents: A Parish Resource.
Edited by Mary Ann Simcoe. Chicago: Liturgy Training Publications, 1985.

Dalmais, I.H., et al. *The Church at Prayer — Volume 1: Principles of The Liturgy.*
Collegeville: Liturgical, 1987.

Duffy, Regis A. *Real Presence.* San Francisco: Harper And Row, 1982.

Fleming, Austin. *Preparing for Liturgy: A Theology and Spirituality.* Washington
D.C.: Pastoral, 1985.

Gelineau, Joseph. *The Liturgy Today and Tomorrow.* London: Darton, Longman,
and Todd, 1978.

Groome, Thomas. *Christian Religious Education.* San Francisco: Harper, 1980.

Keifer, Ralph. *To Give Thanks and Praise.* Washington D.C.: Pastoral, 1980.

Music in Catholic Worship. Washington DC: USCC, 1982.

National Catechetical Directory: Sharing the Light of Faith. Washington DC:
USCC, 1979.

Nelson, John S. "Faith And Adolescents: Insights From Psychology And
Sociology." *Perspectives on Catholic Identity. Network Paper #29.* New
Rochelle: Don Bosco, 1990.

Ostdiek, Gilbert. *Catechesis For Liturgy.* Washington D.C.: Pastoral, 1986.

Power, David N. "Liturgical Praxis: A New Consciousness at the Eye of Worship,"
Worship, 61 (1987): 290.

Shelton, Charles. *Adolescent Spirituality.* Chicago: Loyola UP, 1983.

Strommen, Merton P. *Five Cries of Youth.* San Francisco: Harper, 1974.

A Vision of Youth Ministry. Washington D.C.: USCC, 1986.

Warren, Michael. *Resources For Youth Ministry.* New York: Paulist, 1978.

———. "Culture, Counterculture and the Word," *Liturgy* 6.1 (1986), 85.

———. *Faith, Culture, and the Worshipping Community.* New York: Paulist, 1989.

Whitehead, James D. and Evelyn Eaton. *The Emerging Laity.* Garden City:
Doubleday, 1986.

Chapter 5

Rituals for Adolescence

By John H. Westerhoff, III

ADOLESCENCE

The usefulness of the word teenager - thirteen to nineteen, the junior-senior high school years - is limited. Adolescence, that stage between childhood and adulthood (twelve to twenty-five in our culture) is better, but still inadequate. We can, for the sake of conversation, place persons into groups by chronological age (teenagers), social condition (adolescence) or, as I prefer, developmental style. Only the last makes no specific reference to age. The first is least helpful; no teenager is just like every other - to generalize by age is to fall into error. Adolescence as a social condition or state is more helpful, but only if we are aware that those who are passing through this period in their lives, while facing similar social conditions, live according to various developmental styles, and therefore have various, distinctive needs unrelated to age. That is, there is nothing chronological or natural about maturation, nothing entirely characteristic of any age. While the concept adolescence can be used meaningfully in discussing ritual, developmental style is more helpful, especially as ritual relates to faith.

Faith, as I am using the word, represents the centered activities of persons, embodying their minds (beliefs), hearts (affections) and wills (behaviors), and expressed in their lives according to their growth or development. Faith, as such, is a verb. The activity of "faithing" has no age bounds, but seems to express itself through various identifiable characteristics (styles) at differing points in a person's faith pilgrimage.

For example: A foundational style of faith (I have called it affiliative faith) is typical of childhood, though it is not restricted to those years. Indeed, vast numbers of adults express their faith through this developmental style, either because its needs have not been satisfactorily met or because they have not been provided the necessary encouragement and environment to move beyond it. Still, in one sense, we never appear to grow out of any style of faith, even as our faith expands. That is, the needs of every evolving developmental style remain with us for life, and if we cease to meet those needs, no matter how far our faith has expanded, we will return to this style of faith until its needs are once again met.

Affiliative faith has these characteristics: First and foremost, it is centered in the affections. It is expressed as a religion of the heart, more than of the head or will. Persons with affiliative faith seek their identity in the authority of a community's understandings and ways; similarly, they long for belonging participation and service in the community's life. Dependent upon the community for the content, passion and shape of their faith, persons need to experience and image through ritual and nurture the community's understandings and ways. Through stories told and lived, memories and roots are established; through creative expression the intuition is enhanced and visions of a meaningful future emerge. Through trusting, caring, affirming, accepting interactions, self-worth and identity are framed and the present is made purposeful. Through the sharing of life with those whose past, present and future have depth and purpose, the spiritual life is enhanced.

There is no specific time span, identical for all persons, to satisfy these foundational needs of faith; nor do we ever grow out of their requirements. More than half of all those going through the social condition of adolescence live within the limited perimeters of this faith style, as do many adults. Therefore, our ritual life needs to be expressive of this style of faith and speak to its needs, not only for the sake of those adolescents whose faith is affiliative but for us all, even those of us who have moved beyond its bounds.

Providing that the needs of affiliative faith have been met satisfactorily, sometime during the adolescent years a person can begin to acquire a new style of faith, that is, can begin to expand her or his faith to include new characteristics. I call this new style "searching faith."

Searching faith is marked as a time when the religion of the head begins to predominate over the religion of the heart. The mind begins to search for intellectual justifications of faith. Critical judgement of the community's understandings and ways, as well as short term multiple commitments to ideologies and actions emerge as persons strive to discover what they believe, what it means to give their lives away and live according to their convictions.

Having been "given" an identity during the childhood years, adolescents, in searching faith, struggle to find their own identity and in so doing typically experience the darkness of the soul. Often unverbalized questions such as, Who am I? What communities are worth living in? What causes are worth living for?, dominate life's joyous, troubling, liberating, confusing days and nights. Still persons in searching faith long to belong, especially to a community which shares their concerns for action, critical thought and passion. While they struggle with the authority of the community, they long to respond to new forms of moral, sapiential, charismatic, or personal authority. These are the betwixt and between years, when the social conditions of adolescence, which throw the individual into a state of limbo between childhood and adulthood (a period that can extend from thirteen to thirty), unite with the ordeal and liminality of searching faith. These are the years when it may appear that faith is lost and the community's nurturing has failed. And these are the years when a person one day appears to have matured into adulthood and the next day to have regressed to early childhood. Difficult for both the individual and the community, these years of anxiety and storm must come before faith can assume its fullest dimensions.

Briefly, mature faith, that faith for which we all long, I have named "owned faith." *Owned faith* is the faith of adulthood, but not necessarily of all adults, for it appears that only those who have moved through searching faith can acquire its characteristics of centeredness and personal identity. Indeed, persons with owned faith are secure enough in their convictions to stand against their community of nurture when conscience dictates. Having begun as a heteronomous self and moved to autonomy, the theonomous self emerges. Still in need of community and personally committed to a community's understandings and ways, persons with owned faith reveal themselves to be inner-directed, open to others, but clear and secure in their own faith identity. Concerned to eliminate the dissonances between rhetoric and life, the religion of the will, with its witness to faith, predominated over the religion of heart or mind, although it encompasses both.

Of course owned faith is always expanding; it is not to be understood as a state of arrival or conclusion. New depth and breadth emerge as life's experiences add new dimensions to faith's ever-expanding pilgrimage. Further, the needs and characteristics of earlier styles of faith continue.

For example, doubt and the intellectual quest never end. Nor do the need to belong, the nurturing of the affections, or the place of authority disappear, though they will express themselves somewhat differently. And remember, if these various faith needs are not met, the person with owned faith will return to earlier needs until they are once again satisfied. Thus faith is never static.

Some conclusions. Adolescence is a social condition of youth which must be taken seriously; however, to do so we need to acknowledge the various and distinctive developmental styles of faith which this period in life can encompass. Adolescents have no one set of faith needs. Indeed, they share needs with children and adults. If maturation were the rule, the social condition of adolescence would correspond with the developmental style of searching faith. However, for this correspondence to occur a series of foundational needs must have been met. Since this is rarely the case, persons may be facing the social conditions of adolescence while living in search of affiliative faith. Therefore, the needs of affiliative faith need to be central to the Church's ritual.

For example, to grow into searching faith, persons need to have been given a sense of self-esteem and worth. They need to have learned to accept their strengths and weaknesses, to live in the hope that they will continue to grow, and to possess self-confidence. They need to have learned that they are adequate to meet the future. Hopefully, during the childhood years persons will have experienced the grace of God in a sacramental community where the authority of the Word and the conviction that Jesus is Lord is lived in the intimacy of a belonging, caring fellowship. To have a sense of oneness with God, to feel loved for nothing, to know that you are understood and valued are the gifts of a Christian community. However, for many adolescents, even those brought up in the Church, the experience of loneliness, self-hatred, family conflict, estrangement, insecurity, closed-minded, dogmatic, structural authority and an affectionless environment have made searching faith difficult to attain. In spite of their adolescent social condition, they need a community which nurtures affiliative faith.

Those, however, who have begun to move into searching faith need a community of social concern and action, a community whose ritual unites head and heart with a concern for justice, a community in which critical intellectual judgement is encouraged, doubt affirmed and experimentation permitted. In some cases persons have been forced out of the Church in order to meet these needs. This is especially unfortunate, for these persons still need belonging participation in a passionate community secure in its story and ways.

RITUAL

Ritual is an essential aspect of all life. Indeed, it is our orderly, predictable, repetitive symbolic actions which give life shape and form, meaning and purpose. Without ritual we lack a means for building and establishing community, identity and at-oneness in the world; we are without a means for making the changes in our lives meaningful and integrating, and we are devoid of our most significant means for sustaining and transmitting our understandings and ways. Indeed, there is no cultural choice between ritual or no ritual, but only of what our rituals will be. Ritual is foundational to life. In those historic moments when the Church had lost its soul, it neglected its ritual. Correspondingly, every reform in the history of the Church has been at its core a reformation of ritual. When our rituals change, our lives change, and when we change our understandings and ways, we change our rituals.

Today is marked by new life in the community of faith. The prophets, as of old, have confronted us with the inadequacy of our rituals. Experimentation and change are all about. While necessary in this transitory period marked by a new consciousness of the Gospel's call for justice and community, we also long to secure ourselves in a sanctioned and valued structure of orderly, repetitive actions symbolic of our radical faith. The days of improvisation and change need to end, for in our secular, alien world, the community of renewed, reformed faith needs to establish new structured rituals if it is to maintain its soul.

The chief problem for life in a pluralistic, secular, technological, urban world is attaining, owning, and maintaining one's identity as a person and as a follower of Jesus Christ. The claims for loyalty are legion and the diverse communities which ask our allegiance are many. Only an identity-conscious, tradition-bearing community, rich in meaningful ritual, can help us to know and remember who we are. Life is fragmented and compartmentalized. We search for wholeness and at-oneness in what can be an alienating world. Vital community rituals alone can prevent us from spiritual dislocation and lostness.

The Church cannot live with rituals that divide the generations as if they had nothing in common. We cannot afford to accept the separation of children, youth, and adults for distinctive rituals. Community is the gift of shared rituals. Needs of various persons may differ, but we grow only when we interact with those differences. Peer group isolation prevents growth. When we permit our rites of community to address the needs of some particular group alone, everyone suffers. The norm for the Church's community rite is the Eucharist which, by its very nature, is inclusive of all.

The current craze in which everyone is encouraged to create their own rituals for their own group is divisive. The function of community rites is to form unity, not division. Besides, each generation needs the insights, experiences, and contributions of the others if any are to grow. We need to conserve a memory and maintain a tradition, just as we need to nurture visions and incarnation of futuristic expressions. Without both continuity and change, we cannot maintain security and identity in the present. If our community rituals have ignored the needs of any generation, or have been dominated by any particular generation, they need to be reformed and reshaped until all feel at home in them and all are stretched to newness of faith and life. My point is simple; we do not need special rites of community for adolescents, but we do need a place in our regular community rituals that speaks to adolescents.

RITES OF LIFE CRISIS

There is, however, another category of rites which I prefer to call *rites of life* crisis. Instead of following the calendar as rites of community do, these rites address the changes of our lives. Some correspond to biological changes such as birth, puberty, and death, and others to social changes such as marriage, graduation, and retirement. Such moments of changed role or status are traumatic to both individuals and the community. Ritual aids us to make these changes purposeful; they reestablish order in the community, and help others to understand the possibility and meaning of change.

As such, these rites comprise three distinctive stages, marked at the beginning and at the close by a ceremonial. The first stage is separation. It is followed by a period of transition, a state of liminality during which one learns the skill, awareness, and knowledge essential to one's newly emerging state or role. In the ordeal of this betwixt and between period a unique sense of community develops, and then one is ceremonially reincorporated into the community.

The Church has yet to address satisfactorily the many culturally-new changes in role and status which have emerged in our century. These changes involve every age, for example, retirement for the elderly and continual moves for children. Perhaps more significant, however, are the changes of adolescence. Consider a driver's license, graduation, a first date, job decisions, and many more. Until we explore these biological and social changes of adolescence and address them through meaningful rituals, none will be fully informed by Christian understandings. As a result, adolescence for the church person will become increasingly troubling, and life increasingly segmented, ruptured and secularized.

Third, and from my perspective the most important rituals of all, I prefer to call *rites of identity*. These transition rites are similar to rites of life crisis and are sometimes known as initiation rites. Presently they include baptism, first communion, and confirmation. Celebrated as a single act at birth or adulthood, or spread out over time, these are the rites used by the Church to aid in the formation of Christian identity. Among contemporary Christians confusion reigns over these rituals, their significance and their place in the Church's life.

We have inherited from the Middle Ages a dismembered initiation rite which has tended to make of confirmation a rite of passage into adult, mature, personal, owned faith. While liturgists argue against the delay of confirmation as disruptive of the rite of initiation, I would argue that, in any case, a rite of commitment is misplaced in adolescence. For those adolescents still in affiliative faith such a rite is at best expressive of an affective need to belong to a community and to accept its authority. As such, it functionally stultifies the pilgrimage of faith and encourages immature faith.

Adolescence is a proper time to encourage doubt, questioning, critical judgement, the intellectual quest, and experimentation. A rite of public confirmation of belief and commitment to radical Christian life puts closure on this essential stage in the development of faith. If we are to take faith, ritual and the adolescent seriously, the Church will need to develop a new rite for this important turning point in a person's quest for Christian identity. What is needed is a ritual to aid and encourage the transition from affiliative to searching faith during the adolescent years.

ADOLESCENCE AND RITUAL

Now for some prescriptions consistent with our analysis of adolescence and ritual.

First. Adolescents share with all others a need for intergenerational rites of community. While having some needs special to their social condition and developmental stage, they also have needs identical with others. We grow into maturity insofar as our specific needs are met and insofar as we are provided with role models and experiences which enable us to grow. The generations need to be united in a common ritual which addresses their diverse and changing needs. Only then will persons grow to mature faith and the community remain united. This implies a serious questioning of both our older, rigid, stereotyped, adult-oriented rituals which alienated children and adolescents and our newer innovative attempts at relevance through the separation of the generations and the creation of particular rituals for children, adolescents, and adults.

Persons passing through searching faith have particular needs which the Church's ritual must address, needs which those with owned faith share and to which those with affiliative faith need exposure if they are to grow. (A similar contention can be made in terms of those in affiliative or owned faith.) Reason and the intellect have a place in the Church's ritual. The Word of God addresses our minds as well as our hearts and wills. The sermon (homily) historically has addressed this need and therefore should once again assume a more central role in the Church's Eucharistic ritual. (Parenthetically, that does not mean that a sermon is to be devoid of passion or bore us with intellectualism for twenty minutes.) But rather than isolate any one aspect of our ritual, let us consider how each aspect of the structure might speak to the needs of those in searching faith. (Isolating this one style of faith for consideration is only for the purposes of example. Our community rituals, to be whole, must speak also to the needs of affiliative and owned faith. Only then will they truly meet the needs of adolescents.)

To gather in the name of the Lord in our secular age is in part to confront us with the dissonance between the Church's life and the Gospel. To be called to live under the judgment and inspiration of the Gospel to the end that God's will is done and God's community comes is not easy. Searching faith's need for critical judgment can be addressed at the very beginning of our community ritual. Searching faith's need for visions and dreams can be supplied through our hearing of God's word, though our imaginations will surely not be enhanced if the lessons are passionlessly read. While searching faith may not be able to respond to God's word with a statement of faith, the only way to live meaningfully with doubt is to stand in the presence of those who acclaim the community's faith. Searching faith's unique gift of sensibility and concern for the outsider can then aid the community in its prayers of intercession, saving them from individualized introspection. Further, searching faith's needs for commitment and action can be adequately served by the challenge of the offering which asks us to take up our cross and follow after our Lord Jesus Christ. Further, who more than the person in searching faith, filled with doubt, needs the nurturing grace and acceptance of God given at the Eucharist? At the same time, who can better contribute to the visionary victory party of the people of God?

Others with their differing styles of faith will bring other gifts and each aspect of the ritual can address our various needs. United in a new reformed community ritual, the Church can witness to its faith, address the needs of persons in their faith pilgrimage and equip and stimulate the community to live its faith in an alien world.

Second. There are numerous significant life events in the lives of adolescents which need to be celebrated. Some which come to mind are the acquisition of a driver's license and sometimes a car, a first job, a new school, graduation, a move, a first date and sometimes marriage, leaving home and, for some, their first full-time job. The community of faith needs to celebrate these moments, with the opportunities and responsibilities they entail. Adolescents need to understand the meaning of purposeful work and the nature of vocation; they need to understand their sexuality and the full possibilities of human interaction; they need to understand the issues of freedom and responsibility which come with the power of a driver's license and a car. They need the assistance of meaningful rites of life crisis so that they, their parents, and others who relate with them can be prepared for and live purposefully as Christians in their newly emerging status and roles.

The Church needs to develop new rites which celebrate these days in the lives of persons from the perspective of Christian faith. The Church needs also to provide a means within these rites for learning how to live in their new status or role as follower of Jesus Christ. More than likely this learning would be informal as would the ceremonials which would surround them. More than likely these peer group-oriented rituals would be characterized by improvisation.

Unless we can find ritual ways, within the context of the Christian Church, to aid persons during these years to relate their faith and doubts to the changes in their chronological age and social condition, we will have difficulty being able to aid them in their more important pilgrimage of faith.

Third. Most significant from my perspective are the sacramental rites of identity. Recall the problem I described previously with adolescent confirmation. What the Church needs more than anything else is a new ritual for adolescence. It will take time for it to gain acceptance and emerge, but let me suggest what it might become.

At an inquiry retreat where adolescents between thirteen and nineteen might be exposed to what I am calling a covenant of discipleship rite and its ordeal of preparation, both those who decide to prepare and those who do not can be affirmed and blessed. Following this event, those who have decided to prepare for this step in their faith pilgrimage should come before the congregation with their parents to announce their intentions. A group of adolescents who have recently completed this rite and a few chosen adults of owned faith might be called forth from the congregation and assigned the task of assisting them in their preparation.

A series of learnings necessary for searching faith needs to be established. When it is completed (no more than one year but perhaps less), the person is prepared to make her or his covenant of discipleship. Some of these learnings would include the skills of biblical exegesis and interpretation; an awareness of the lives of the saints, their struggles with the faith and their darkness of the soul; and a knowledge of how one can best learn about other religions and expressions of faith. One further set of learnings might include a knowledge of God's vision for the Church, an honest awareness of the Church's condition today, and some skills for institutional reform.

Prepared persons might present themselves before the congregation on St. Thomas's Day and after giving an account of their preparation, make a covenant with God and the Church to be a learner, that is, one who will take full responsibility for his or her own faith even as they critically struggle with the faith into which they had been nurtured. At the same ritual, these persons' parents might pray a prayer of gratitude to God for taking away from them the full burden of responsibility for their children's faith. The congregation further can celebrate this new and important stage in the person's faith pilgrimage and offer their support, encouragement and aid.

A new ritual for adolescence such as this could be a most significant innovation in the ritual life of the Church. It would provide an important aid to a person's maturing pilgrimage of faith, and also to the Church's call to be a radical community of faith in-but-not-of-the-world.

CONCLUSION

In conclusion, let me suggest that most of the attempts at bringing the ritual life of the Church and adolescence together are not radical enough. On the one hand, our attempts at relevant community rituals for adolescents that separate them from other generations are an error. On the other hand, our unwillingness to develop truly new and unique transitional identity and life crisis rites for adolescents is also a grave mistake. We have not thought radically enough. My hope is while this essay may prove wrong in its conclusions, it has at least driven our discussion to the foundation. Time will tell. I trust the colloquy has begun.

BIBLIOGRAPHY

Additional works by John H.Westerhoff, III, on the themes of faith
development, worship/liturgy, and ritual:

Westerhoff, John. *Will Our Children Have Faith?* New York: Seabury, 1976.

——————. *Bringing Up Children in the Christian Faith.* Minneapolis: Winston, 1980.

——————. *Building God's People in a Materialistic Society.* New York: Seabury,
1983.

——————. *Living the Faith Community.* San Francisco: Harper, 1985.

Westerhoff, John and Gwen Kennedy Neville. *Generation to Generation.*
Philadelphia: Pilgrim, 1974.

——————. *Learning through Liturgy.* New York: Seabury, 1978.

Westerhoff, John and William Willimon. *Liturgy and Learning through the Life
Cycle.* New York: Seabury, 1980.

Part II

Preparing Liturgical and Worship Experiences

Overview

Part Two of this book provides you with guidelines, processes, and key elements for preparing liturgical and worship experiences with youth. Also included is an extensive resource guide covering theological resources, liturgical preparation resources, youth worship resources, and resource materials for liturgical celebrations.

Tom Tomaszek begins Part Two with an essay on preparing and evaluating worship with youth. He begins by developing key insights for celebrating worship with adolescents, including an analysis of the relationship between liturgy (using the *Directory of Masses with Children)* and catechesis (using *The Challenge of Adolescent Catechesis)* and the need for liturgical catechesis. In the second part of his essay, Tomaszek outlines six steps toward preparing and evaluating worship with youth.

Gilbert Ostdiek utilizes several key church documents to develop a set of qualities and criteria for effective liturgy. His essay is a tool to determine the key qualities you seek in a liturgy that is pastorally effective for young people.

Kathleen Fischer proposes three helpful guidelines for reading reflecting and reflecting on scripture, especially as you prepare liturgical celebrations. She writes that we need to (1) to attend carefully to the text itself, (2) call on historical and literary criticism for assistance, and (3) celebrate and live the text within a community of faith.

Michael Moynahan describes and illustrates seven types of liturgical drama that you can use: interpretive proclamation, group interpretive proclamation, mime or pantomine, improvisation, psycho-drama, scenario or story dramatization, and total dramatic liturgical experience.

Pat Schaffran and **Pat Kozak** provide critical considerations that liturgical planners need to become aware of as they prepare worship experiences. In their first essay they provide a well-rounded understanding of symbols and rituals and practical examples of how to develop holistic experiences. In their second essay they describe the impact of language on liturgy and specific directions for the development of inclusive language in all celebrations. In their third essay they challenge liturgical experiences to respect and appreciate cultural diversity and become inclusive of the variety of cultural traditions, symbols, art, music.

Edward Foley outlines the similarities between the two communal rites of Penance (Form II and III) and then outlines their strengths and limitations of the two communal rites. He then offers several key principles for communal celebration of the rites of Penance and three examples of how the principles and rites can be used.

Chapter 6

Preparing and Evaluating Worship for Youth

By Thomas N. Tomaszek

INTRODUCTION

In Chapter Four, "Improving Worship for Youth," I discussed worship as liturgy and life—an expression of the covenant relationship between God and humans. Worship accomplishes the two-fold action of glorifying God and sanctifying those assembled in God's name as the Body of Christ. Liturgy celebrates the paschal mystery of God's saving action in our lives and calls the community to become the ongoing presence of Christ in the world.

Using the language and dynamics of relationships, I tried to articulate the difficulties that young people may have in becoming part of the worshipping community as it gathers for its weekly Eucharistic liturgy. Some of these problems arise from the developmental tasks of adolescence which cause youth to withdraw from active participation. Other difficulties are attributable to the assembly's inattentiveness to itself—including youth or those not from the dominant culture. The lack of liturgical catechesis available to all age groups since the reforms of Vatican II also contributes to the confusion regarding roles and responsibilities at liturgy leading to the inability of communities to improve the worship experience for its members.

I suggested two models for achieving youth participation in the community's worship. First, those responsible for preparing liturgy need to implement ways the assembly has of attending to its young people and of adapting the rites to include their forms of expression. Secondly, creative Eucharistic and non-Eucharistic liturgical experiences for youth in peer groups will serve to improve youth participation in the community's celebrations. I listed a number of ideas for responding to these goals including a re-evaluation of the other community-building and outreach efforts of the parish's youth ministry effort, since these endeavors have a significant effect on adolescents' readiness for ritual.

PREPARING AND EVALUATING WORSHIP FOR YOUTH

With the ideas and suggestions of that previous article as a foundation, I wish to focus on the principles and practices by which we can prepare and evaluate worship for youth. Here I choose to follow Austin Fleming's well-articulated language distinction between planning and preparing for liturgy. [1] If words name our action, then we should be about the task of preparing for liturgy, rather than *planning* it. Rituals, by their nature, have a predictable content and form. Liturgy, as ritual worship, has a predictable content and form which demands more attention to preparing the setting, environment and assembly than it necessitates a "reinvention" of its rites on a regular basis. It's my intention to offer specific suggestions later in this article for the formation of a liturgy preparation committee which includes youth and youth concerns.

My thesis for principles by which we can prepare and evaluate worship for youth begins with a re-discovery of the *Directory for Masses with Children*. This document, which was published in 1973, later precipitated the three Eucharistic prayers for use on such occasions when children comprise the majority of the assembly. My intention is to show that the developmental needs of adolescents are no less deserving of particular liturgical adaptations. In concept, the *Directory* establishes a pastoral adaptation of the Roman Rite for "...baptized children who have yet to be fully initiated through the sacrament of confirmation and eucharist..." (#1). Norms for adapting liturgy to the needs of particular groups, regions, and peoples are addressed in the *Constitution on the Sacred Liturgy* "provided the substantial unity of the Roman Rite is preserved". (#38)

One may infer the intent of that paragraph of the *Constitution* was to allow liturgy to adapt to the changing cultural considerations which will always affect the celebration of the rites. Liturgy is always influenced by the cultural environment in which it takes place, but also by the predisposition and readiness of those who participate. It would seem that the *Directory* has both these influences in mind as it makes its pastoral suggestions.

Those of us who are concerned with the faith development of adolescent and pre-adolescent youth might make a rather "legalistic" argument for including those ages groups—by definition—as included in those "not fully initiated" into the faith. I would rather understand the intent of the *Directory* as responding to the *Constitution's* call for attention to the full participation of those assembled for Eucharist. (CSL #14) My aim here is to present sufficient reference to youth ministry theory and other research so as to show the connection between liturgy and catechesis, since one of the aims of adolescent catechesis is the formation and initiation of youth into the community of believers. It is my hope that such a rationale will serve as foundation for a critical re-reading of the *Directory* and allow me to make pastoral suggestions for adaptation of the rites to respond first, to adolescents' experiences at Eucharistic liturgies, and secondly, to the developmental tasks of adolescence. [2]

CELEBRATING WORSHIP WITH ADOLESCENTS

The scene is Easter Sunday morning and my friends and I are gliding through a meadow on cross-country skis amid the grandeur of the Rocky Mountains. The wind is calm and it is snowing large, spectacularly-lit flakes as the sun pierces through the clouds momentarily. The "whoosh" of our skis gently furrowing through several inches of new powder snow is the only sound heard. No one speaks as the splendor and stillness of the moment are too precious to interrupt. Cresting a small rise in the terrain we instinctively stop to catch our breath—and to capture this breath-taking place forever in our minds. Finally, Cathy breaks the silence as she exclaims, "I feel God alive here, all around us!" The rest of us smile and nod knowingly in agreement.

My companions are several high-school students with whom I have traveled to this Continental Divide ski-area as chaperone. Though we have known each other for some time because of other trips, our experience of the "awe-some" this morning creates a new bond among us. Later, while recalling the scene for another member of the group who remained behind, we drift into a discussion of God's presence in our lives, of our faith and beliefs, and the power of that moment. It's an experience that is permanently etched in my memory.

Ten years later, it is Easter Sunday morning and I am standing at the cantor's podium preparing to lead the assembly in singing the opening hymn "Christ Is Alive." Multicolored light is streaming through the stained glass windows of this immense building, illuminating the brightly-colored new clothing of many people present. For a brief moment, all is silence in anticipation of the organ's triumphant first chord. As I gaze out into the filled-to-capacity church, I seek to make eye contact with as many faces as possible. But my hopeful glances are seldom returned, and as the hymn begins, my gesture to sing adds few voices to join the choir's lead... "Christ is alive, let Christians sing! His cross stands empty to the sky...Alleluia!"

As the hymn continues, my eyes focus on the face of a teen-aged youth, whose drifting gaze is toward someplace other than here and now. Arms crossed as he stands a somewhat defiant distance from his mother, the sport coat and tie he is wearing for this festive occasion seem inconsistent with his disposition. A distressed look fills the mother's face. Trying not to notice, I shift my attention to another part of the congregation, but the scene has distracted me from my task. I can't help but feel a twinge of the frustration evident in the faces of both mother and child.

These two personal recollections of Easter Sunday, while not parallel as liturgical experiences, do help to describe the reality of worshipping with and ministering to adolescents. For many youth, the community's worship is oftentimes only a distraction to be endured, though other experiences, especially in nature, may implicitly trigger a faith-filled response on their part. The range of participation by adolescents present in the assembly is likely to match the widest spectrum of possibilities. Those not present account for an even greater percentage of the responses.

I could have also described—in much too vivid detail—the behavior of two high-energy four-year-olds sitting in the front pew that same Easter morning, as well as the embarrassed look on their mothers' faces as each tried to intervene. It is this slightly younger age-group about whom the *Directory for Masses with Children* is concerned when it states:

> In the upbringing of children in the Church a special difficulty arises from the fact that liturgical celebrations, especially the eucharist, cannot fully exercise their inherent pedagogical force upon children...Nonetheless, we may fear spiritual harm if over the years children repeatedly experience in the Church things that are barely comprehensible... (DMC #2)

Though "the *Directory* is concerned with children who have not yet entered the period of preadolescence". (DMC #2), I believe a similar concern for "spiritual harm" to adolescents is also warranted by repeated poor liturgical experiences. The *Directory* outlines a pastoral response for adapting liturgy to the developmental faith expressions of children. In recognizing those developmental needs which preclude children from entering actively into the community's worship, the document leads us to an awareness of the process of initiation whereby children are welcomed into our assemblies and grow in faith. It's basic concern for children as children makes it a unique document of the Roman Church, and its consideration of potential "spiritual harm" establishes its inclusion of a pastoral response.[3]

While adolescents are certainly more able than young children to comprehend the community's liturgies in which they partake, developmentally youth are still at a vulnerable stage of faith. The incomprehension may be more on the part of adults and parents as they struggle to understand the mood swings and latest fads of youth. In its opening paragraph, *The Challenge of Adolescent Catechesis* describes this stage of faith not in negative terms but as offering our communities a unique opportunity:

> All human beings experience change during adolescence. This change can be exciting if it awakens a deeper sense of self-identity, leads to the expansion of authentic freedom, enhances our ability to relate to others, and promotes greater maturity. However, the changes of adolescence can also be depressing, alienating and filled with self-doubt and anxiety. Precisely because of the many divergent possibilities, the time of adolescence is a unique opportunity for the Catholic Christian community to affirm, support, and challenge young people to grow as persons and believers. *(Challenge 3)*

We may refer to such youth ministry here as a "challenge," but those who are charged with coordinating this responsibility on behalf of the community know it as a complex task of melding complementary ministries to, with, by, and for young people. Since *A Vision for Youth Ministry* was published in 1976, the role of youth ministers in developing the faith of adolescents has gradually shifted away from an image that they are some sort of "folksy pied pipers" who lead youth to a responsible Christian life. Today's youth ministers, who are more frequently full-time paid professionals with training and experience in the tasks of adolescent faith development, understand the important role the whole community plays in creating a healthy environment for its young people. A comprehensive vision of youth ministry includes the components of word, worship, community, guidance and healing, justice and service, enablement and advocacy.[4]

Each of these seven components when present in the community's life complements the total outreach to young people, and conversely, when they are done poorly or are neglected detract from the overall effort. To understand this dynamic is to realize that a Sunday liturgy cannot be the only time of the week we welcome young people in our parishes (Community). Similarly, assisting youth in becoming Christian leaders (Enablement) will not occur without challenging them to live a life of outreach and compassion for the poor and unjustly treated (Justice and Service). Likewise, we cannot stand for and with youth (Advocacy) without listening to their pain and walking with them as they strive for wholeness (Guidance and Healing). And we cannot speak about the Word or preach the Good News without a willingness to enter into young people's lives as Christ so entered the world as the Word made flesh (Word). When we lose sight of the connection between liturgy and the other dimensions of the community's life and prayer (Worship), we risk the "spiritual harm" of young people alluded to in the *Directory*.

IMPLICATIONS FOR LITURGICAL PREPARATION

Preparing to celebrate liturgy with adolescents, first and foremost, requires that we pay attention to their needs and faith development. This occurs in a variety of ways but, more than anything, youth ministry is a ministry of spending time. My intention in chaperoning my students' ski trip was not to have a meaningful dialogue about the existence of God. But our common experience enabled that sharing to take place. I wish I could say that I preconceived such a marvelous experience would take place, but I did not know then what I know now. Preparing youth to help at meal programs, assist the elderly, serve the handicapped, demonstrate for peace, listen to their peers who are addicted to drugs and alcohol, and sharing those experiences with them will afford plenty of "spontaneous" moments for theological reflection. I am convinced that those opportunities, as well as other formal opportunities of faith sharing and catechesis, will become the basis for greater participation in Eucharist as well as form a desire in youth for greater knowledge of the Catholic Christian tradition and beliefs.

Secondly, preparing for liturgy involves attending to the relationships we have with young people and which they have with one another and with God. Because people are capable of continual development, so are their relationships with God. *(Sharing the Light of Faith* #173) Don Kimball describes this process as "spiritual direction" whereby we help youth "get in touch or back in touch with God." By encouraging youth to listen, and then, discern a response to God's movement in their lives, we will *educate* (lead towards something or someone) them in the ways of our faith. (Kimball 127) Our actions need to respect adolescents' desire for independence and self-determination. "They (adolescents) mirror what they have learned from family, parish, and school, yet they strongly insist that they are working out their own faith. They are in transit, on a journey, and they are open to us joining them—provided we don't try to map it all out for them." (Nelson 4)

Finally, preparing to celebrate liturgy which reflects adolescents' faith and feelings will require catechesis. "It should include the study of the Gospels, of the nature of the Church and liturgy, of the way in which the Church celebrates its union with Christ in the Eucharist, and the liturgy's intimate relationship to life, faith, doctrine, and the Church. The meaning of symbols, of bread, wine, and faith community, is probed." *(Sharing the Light of Faith #136)* Effective catechesis, grounded in a comprehensive approach to youth ministry, will gradually introduce young people to the rich liturgical traditions of the Church.

THE RELATIONSHIP BETWEEN
LITURGY AND ADOLESCENT CATECHESIS

Catechesis is intrinsically linked with the whole of liturgical and sacramental activity, for it is in the sacraments, especially in the Eucharist, that Christ Jesus works in fullness for the transformation of human beings. *(Catechesi Tradendae #23)*

The intrinsic link between catechesis and liturgy of which John Paul II speaks calls us to further examine how the aims of adolescent catechesis may also influence liturgical preparation. There are five foundational principles articulated in *The Challenge of Adolescent Catechesis:*

1) Adolescent catechesis is situated within the lifelong developmental process of faith growth and of ongoing catechesis.
2) Adolescent catechesis fosters Catholic Christian faith in the three dimensions of trusting, believing, and doing.
3) Adolescent catechesis supports and encourages the role of the family and, in particular, the role of the parent in the faith growth of the young person.
4) Adolescent catechesis respects the unique cultural heritages of young people while at the same time engaging young people in examining their culture in the light of faith and examining their faith in the light of culture.
5) Adolescent catechesis is integrated and developed within a comprehensive, multifaceted approach to ministry with youth. *(Challenge 9)*

Much psychological and sociological research has been done to describe and define the stages of development and growth. In particular, *The Challenge* defines younger adolescents as ranging from ages 11/12 - 14/15, and older adolescents from ages 14/15 - 18/19. Even a cursory reading of the above foundational principles (referred to in parentheses here) yields some significant observations for how we might ritually celebrate faith with each of these age groups. At a time when adolescents believe they are breaking away from their parents' control (principle #3), their behaviors are readily influenced by peers, the media, and other significant adults in their lives. Don Kimball suggests that adolescents have only shifted that control from one outside force to another, that they are not free at all. (Kimball 123)

Liturgically, that would seem to support the significance of peer group liturgies and opportunities to participate in parish liturgies in the company of friends and peers.

The Challenge also suggests the importance of integrating the signs, symbols, and images of youth culture into the catechetical program (principle #4). Liturgy, as symbolic activity, offers meaningful ways to challenge and affirm those cultural symbols in the light of the Catholic Christian tradition. As part of a comprehensive outreach, liturgy recognizes the struggles of adolescents, celebrates the passages in life stages, and offers spiritual direction.

Liturgy, as part of a comprehensive outreach to young people (principle #5) is only possible if youth are ready for the ritual experience of liturgy. Frequently, youth are not able to enter into the symbols which unite the adult community of faith. The bread and wine, the songs and prayers, the person of the minister, and the assembly itself as ritual symbols are not engaging to adolescents wishing to "distance" themselves from their parents' and community values as a way of self-identification. When that happens the "diabolic" nature of those symbols becomes operative in adolescents experience of faith. "This failure can also emerge from ministers' and parents' lack of any real interest in youth culture. Difficult as this often is, young people need to be known through their identifying symbols and enthusiasm if they are to be realistically included in the adult community." (Philibert 96)

One of the first tasks of maturing in faith (principle #1), therefore achieving a readiness for ritual, is to enter into the symbolic activity in adult ways. This may involve abandoning or moving away from images of God which no longer fully describe the faith relationship, and replacing them with more appropriate images. Paul Philibert suggests that a familiar scenario of adolescence is appropriating an image of an "Alienating God" who asks worthless acts of self-denial and unquestioned conformity. This is reinforced by parents and other adults making a big issue of their non-attendance at Sunday liturgy. (Philibert 102)

Catechetically, we can enable youth to image God as One who recognizes and affirms us in our uniqueness as members of the Body of Christ. Pastorally, this is accomplished best through individual relationships, small group experiences, and other, more personal outreaches to youth (Principle #2). Seen in this light, the relationship between catechesis and liturgy suggests that peer group and small group liturgical experiences, such as often happen on retreats and days of reflections, are likely to be more effective in enabling the faith development of adolescents through challenging their negative images of God. Many of us have observed the effectiveness of these experiences. It's important to understand why they are effective, and more so, appropriate.

PARALLELS IN THE DIRECTORY
FOR MASSES WITH CHILDREN

In examining the general principles of the *Directory of Masses with Children*, we find a number of significant parallels to the foundational principles of adolescent catechesis. The Rev. Virgil Funk discusses seven principles which may be identified in the first chapter of the document. (Funk)

The first principle is that a fully Christian life requires living the paschal mystery through participation in liturgy as an assembly. He suggests that active participation does not imply only singing or not singing, but a willingness to have one's life transformed by the ritual. Additionally, not all liturgy is Eucharistic, but it should all be implicitly paschal, that is, symbolic of the passage from death to life. For adolescents emerged in the developmental passage to adulthood, liturgy should be the expression of faith as well as the means for deepening it. *(Sharing the Light of Faith* #113)

The second principle is that all who have a part in the formation of children should consult and work together. Giving a variety of reasons why this is important, including the child's experience of communal activity, a meal of friendship, and of the community's expression of gratitude, the Directory provides us with a clear link to the tasks of catechesis: message, community, worship, and service. The bond between the liturgy and catechesis is increased when we call forth the entire community's responsibility for each.

The third principle is that the Christian family has the greatest role in teaching human values. Here we find a direct correlation to the third foundational principle of adolescent catechesis which also reaffirms the role of parents and family in supporting and encouraging faith growth.

The fourth principle calls for the Christian community to exercise its responsibility for children by giving witness to the Gospel in word and deed. The idealism of adolescents makes them very sensitive to the phoniness evident in the "do as I say, not as I do" philosophy of some parents and adults. Catechists frequently complain about the lack of support which occurs when parents of youth do not regularly participate in the sacraments.

The fifth principle suggests that catechetical programs be directed towards the Mass (which I would re-interpret to include all liturgical experiences). Gil Ostdiek's distinction between catechesis *through* liturgy and catechesis *for* liturgy is helpful. Both types of catechesis are important to the faith of adolescents who are searching for meaning and defining their identity through relationships. Ostdiek's catechetical method involves three steps: *attending* to what and how we actually experience at liturgy, *reflecting* on what our experience means, and *applying* what we have learned to future celebrations of liturgy. (Ostdiek 17)

The sixth principle cautions us to avoid "didactic" celebrations. Recent catechetical theory emphasizes the importance of "experiential" learning models for all ages of faith development. It would seem we need to break away from the "classroom approach" to liturgy as well. An illustration of how this approach occurs is when prepared "themes" overwhelm or obscure the central theme of all eucharistic liturgies—namely, the paschal mystery. A non-didactic use of theme allows it to focus the assembly's attention on particular aspects of the mysteries. Because of the rich symbolic nature of all liturgy, we risk destroying its effectiveness when we try to explain, rather than interpret and reflect upon, the operative symbols present when youth worship. The experience of good liturgies will have a catechizing effect upon those present.

The seventh principle considers that everything should be aimed at the response of the child. Here Funk is concerned that "We have forgotten that the formation of character is prior to the education of conscience. Orthodoxy has overshadowed ortho-praxis." Good liturgy challenges all present in the assembly to go forth in a renewed spirit of Christian commitment including adolescents who are "trying on" this tradition handed on to them by their parents and sponsors at baptism. This would suggest that service opportunities and reflection on the issues of peace and justice play a significant role in catechesis of youth, as well as their preparedness for liturgy.

In conclusion, if we understand the intrinsic link between all liturgy and catechesis, we can be confident that the best liturgies will celebrate the faith experiences of Christian believers, and in turn, create another faith experience.

FIVE GENERAL IMPLICATIONS

In addition to the implied need for liturgical catechesis, I would identify five general implications of the Directory for Masses with Children as seen in the light of adolescent catechetical theory:

First, that parishes provide opportunities for youth to celebrate liturgy in peer groups and in small groups. (The notion of small groups might also include occasions which are inter-generational, yet promote a more "intimate" atmosphere.)

Second, that a variety of non-eucharistic liturgical experiences be celebrated with young people, in addition to opportunities for eucharistic liturgy. These experiences might follow the rhythm of the school calendar or be integrated into catechetical efforts based on the faith themes suggested in *The Challenge of Adolescent Catechesis*.

Third, that adults involved in preparing youth liturgical experiences be knowledgeable of and familiar with the dimensions of youth culture so as to integrate current issues and artistic styles into the liturgy, and to enable youth to examine culture through liturgical expression.

Fourth, that adults involved in preparing the community's liturgies take seriously their responsibility to adapt liturgy to the faith expressions of all present in the assembly, and that catechetical and pastoral personnel advocate for youth when this does not occur.

Fifth, that opportunities be established for youth to prepare liturgy for their peers and to be involved in the preparation of the community's liturgy. This might include establishment of apprenticeship programs for the liturgical ministries.

STEPS TOWARD PREPARING AND EVALUATING WORSHIP FOR YOUTH

In the preceding pages I have tried to present a rationale for preparing youth and the community for worship as the first task of preparing for the worship experience itself. I move now to a consideration of the particular responsibilities of preparing for liturgy. Austin Fleming's *Preparing for Liturgy* is an extremely helpful resource. In it he describes six basic tasks involved in preparing for eucharistic liturgy: (1) Prepare a place where the community gathers for worship, (2) Prepare for the proclamation of the scriptures, (3) Prepare the music of praise and prayer, (4) Prepare the table and the table prayer, (5) Prepare bread and wine, a simple meal, (6) Prepare a moment that invites the community to prayer and helps ready believers for communion with the Lord and one another. (Fleming 37)

To prepare the time, place, Word, music, table, and gifts which will become elements of the community's worship is a responsibility which requires as much intuitive sense as it does necessary skill and knowledge of resources. Fleming makes a point that the balancing of creative intuition and basic skills makes the task of preparing for liturgy akin to an art form, but that the liturgical arts have no usefulness except in the enabling of the community's worship. I heartily agree and add a concern for apprenticing youth who either demonstrate an affinity for the liturgical arts or express a desire to learn them. Not only will these youth provide ideas and energy to the preparation of youth liturgies, but they will likely continue to assist the community's celebrations in the years to come. *(Sharing the Light of Faith #121)*

STEP ONE: GATHERING THOSE WHO WILL PREPARE

Generally speaking, the following people should regularly be involved in preparing liturgy, including those worship times specifically for youth:

* presider
* the parish liturgy coordinator
* the music director or choir leader
* the liturgical ministries coordinator
* representatives of the assembly.

Since more than one of the above-mentioned roles often are accounted for by the same individual, it is difficult to suggest a total number of persons who should be involved. The answer is, generally, as many as will be needed to accomplish all the tasks necessary, and who can provide the insights and leadership for the preparation. Of particular importance is including sufficient representatives of the assembly so that the liturgy preparation team will enjoy a creative dialogue of suggestions and input when it makes decisions and selections. *(Directory for Masses with Children #29)*.

When preparing for youth liturgy (few adults present), the same list of individuals should be considered for the preparation team. The only change might be to give greater attention to involving additional members of the group who will serve as liturgical ministers.

This raises the question of whether youth should be part of parish liturgy committees. The answer is emphatically, YES! Many parishes have considered or tried involving youth in a liturgy committee, but have encountered problems or apathy. Generally, the difficulties arise from failing to provide the necessary formation, support, and encouragement adolescents need to successfully participate in adult committees. The scenario is usually something like this: we invite John and Joan to be the youth representatives on the liturgy committee, but John and Joan have never had any formal or informal instruction on what they might need to know about liturgy before they get there. On the night of the first meeting, both of them are a few minutes late because John's dad arrived home late from work and he had agreed to drive the two of them to the meeting. When they arrive, the parish musician and the committee chairperson are bickering over a musical selection which the musician feels is inappropriate for the season. Somewhat at a loss for how to interpret the seriousness of this argument, John and Joan spend most of the evening quietly observing the interactions of the committee members. Towards the end of the meeting, a well-meaning member who has noticed that John and Joan have not said anything, asks them which song they would like to have sung for a recessional. Both shrug their shoulders and say that they are not sure, but anything will be okay with them. "Like, is that the song at the end of the Mass?" Next month, John and Joan decide not to attend the committee meeting because it was boring and it seemed like all anyone did was argue over things which the two of them really did not understand. The committee members do not bother to call John or Joan after they do not show up for the next meeting because it seemed like they were not really interested in preparing liturgy.

I would estimate that this scenario, or something similar, has been played out in far too many parishes (parish council representation is another prime example). The intention of involving youth is good, but no attention is given to preparing youth for the experience or supporting them throughout. In fact, the dynamics operating here which prevent John and Joan from having a positive experience in preparing liturgy are similar to the issues which prevent youth from full participation in the community's worship.

By assigning one adult member of the committee to be John and Joan's contact and mentor, the parish could have demonstrated its concern for youth involvement in liturgy. The contact person's role should be three-fold: first, to provide John and Joan with the necessary background information on liturgy preparation; second, to be their support at the meeting itself, by calling to remind them of the meeting date, time, and place, by offering to drive them to and from the meeting, by sitting next to them during the meeting so that questions could be answered while the meeting is in progress, and by talking to them afterward as a way of "debriefing" the experience. The model is a relational approach to ministry and to leadership development which not only will elicit greater participation of John and Joan in the task of the committee, but will likely serve to develop their faith commitment because they have experienced the personal support and caring of an adult. (I might add that this model of leadership enablement is appropriate for adults as well, and may help to solve the volunteer dilemma that many parishes experience.)

STEP TWO: SETTING THE ENVIRONMENT FOR WORSHIP

The following considerations are of primary importance in establishing the environment in which liturgy will take place:

Season of the Church Year

The liturgical seasons not only influence the broad and subtle expressions which will characterize the liturgy, but also point to events of Jesus' life as they unfold the paschal mystery being commemorated at Eucharist. When preparing for liturgy especially in the seasons of Advent, Christmas, Lent, and Easter, encourage youth to share stories of family traditions and rituals which accompany these feasts and seasons. These cultural experiences will set the tone for creative sharing, and help youth make the connection between ritual worship and the rituals of their daily lives.

Season of the Calendar Year

Though our celebrations of the liturgical seasons are intimately connected to our experience of the seasons of the year, other annual cycles—particularly the school calendar—are of special significance to young people. Do not overlook these opportunities to ritualize such events as homecoming, graduation, or even report card times.

Current Events

If the preparation timeline permits, consider how world, local and parish events may influence the liturgical experience. This might be done not only through the prayers of the faithful, but through other liturgical elements as well. Consider regular ways that special achievements, birthdays, anniversaries and other remembrances can be made part of the celebration.

Spirit of the Assembly

As a liturgist, I have found that assessing the psychological readiness and spirit of those who will be assembled and trying to be sensitive to how their response and active participation will be influenced by those factors is the single most effective way I have of helping to prepare the liturgical environment. Especially for small group or peer group liturgies, begin by answering the question, "What frame of mind, heart, and level of energy are the assembly likely to bring to worship?" The answers will help in determining appropriate musical selections, gestures, and needs for the physical environment.

Physical Environment

The physical space of worship also influences the celebration of the rites. Though you may not have a choice as to which space is used, whether that's a church, auditorium or small chapel or room, other factors such as lighting, seating, ability to hear and see, prevalence of noise and distractions, and even temperature, are likely to have an impact on the worship experience. The energy level of youth, particularly early adolescents, is one factor to keep in mind when preparing the physical space of worship. In non-church or chapel settings, beyond comfort, a consideration of whether this space will give the assembly a "sense of the holy" is a good starting point (DMC #25).

STEP THREE: GATHERING RESOURCES

In order to prepare well, it's necessary to gather all the appropriate resources the group might need for reference. Here are some basics:

* Lectionary and Sacramentary (or bible and liturgical calendar).
* Hymnals or other musical resources.

* List of musicians and their repertoire.
* Artists and artisans who can assist with environment.
* Vessels, candles and other necessities.

In preparing youth liturgies, it will also be helpful to have a collection of poem, prayer and drama references which may inspire creativity for the liturgical situation. Also helpful is a sense of the lyrics to current popular songs, and a reference library of tapes or records which might be used. Much of the current liturgical music which is being created is available on record or tape. Consider these as sources for ideas as well as responses.

STEP FOUR: PUTTING IT ALL TOGETHER

The Directory for Masses with Children makes pastoral suggestions for the areas of offices and ministries, place and time, singing and music, gestures, visual elements and silence. Additionally, it makes specific recommendations for adapting the parts of the Mass. I offer the following combined categories for your consideration in preparing liturgy:

The Word

After determining the readings assigned for the day, feast, or particular liturgical celebration, consider spending some time reflecting about how these scriptural passages are speaking to your faith story at this moment. Share those reflections with one another as a prayer to begin the rest of your preparation. Consider recording or writing those reflections down for the homilist especially if he is not present for the preparation time. (DMC #41)

Music and Song

Music is normative to liturgy, but also is influenced by culture and personal taste. Everyone has a favorite style of contemporary music, but liturgical music serves a different purpose than entertainment. Music at liturgy is an expression of the faith of the assembly, not a performance or listening session. One way to describe the liturgical purpose of music and song is to understand the creative tension by which liturgical music reveals culture and yet must be counter-cultural. Because the style of music sung at liturgy is often the element which most characterizes the celebration and because most people have a clear sense of personal musical taste, that "creative" tension can often dissolve into interpersonal tension and arguments about which music is "appropriate" for liturgy.

The documents *Music in Catholic Worship* and *Liturgical Music Today* are helpful in understanding the function of music at various times within the liturgy and the role of the music ministers. It is important to make the distinction here between liturgies with youth as the primary participants, and the Sunday celebrations of the whole community. One of the best arguments for more opportunities for youth liturgies is to allow for a greater variety of contemporary music to be adapted and used. (DMC #30)

I hope that the arguments made previously in this article have helped to fashion a rationale why youth expressions (including contemporary music) may also have a place in the whole community's celebrations. But the thinking usually goes like this, "Let them play *that* music at the youth liturgy, we have to consider *all* the people present for weekend celebrations." Well, a good percentage of *all* those people present on Sundays and Saturday evenings *are* young people. It is time our celebrations start including their needs and move away from "adult-only" expressions. (DMC #19)

As a liturgical musician, I have listened to countless arguments as to why the music used at liturgy should be "liturgical." Some will argue that secular music, because of its intent to entertain and its connotations of social events, is inadequate for liturgical situations. But I know of no musical argument which is more significant than the need for liturgy to speak from the faith life of the assembly, even while it is in concert with the age-old rituals. *Music becomes liturgical when it is appropriated as an expression of faith.* We may all be able to cite examples of "liturgical" music which for a variety of reasons can never be an expression of faith for us or for youth. (Let those who would stand on soapboxes be required to sing that "traditional" Catholic hymn, "Sons of God.")

My experience has been that popular music often speaks to the faith of youth because it almost exclusively speaks about relationships. Defining self and identity through friends and other relationships is a cornerstone task of adolescence. Admittedly, there are too many examples of lyric and musical suggestiveness in the currently popular styles. Weeds grow amidst the wheat. But to the well-intentioned ear there are always songs which can be used to describe the beauty of God's love and commitment to us. In real terms, little spiritual harm is done by selectively using contemporary songs at youth liturgies. It is my opinion that greater risk comes from celebrating rituals with youth which do not relate to, celebrate, or challenge their life experiences. Popular music is effective in accomplishing those aims.

I have also experienced that most youth (and adults, for that matter) are unaware of the more recent developments in liturgical music and are pleasantly surprised when they hear recordings which make use of the contemporary styles and synthesizers, percussion, and other electronic effects. Thankfully, we are longer limited in our contemporary liturgical music to the folk-rock musical styles of the 60s and 70s which were popular as the first songs in the vernacular were being created. Today's liturgical music demonstrates a blend of innovation and tradition, and a wide use of instrumentation to accompany creatively written texts and settings of the Scriptures. I have included some references to composers and publishers at the end of this chapter which I hope will be of assistance in exploring some of those resources with which you may not be familiar.

I have given this section greater treatment because it is an area of liturgy which receives considerable attention. Finally, may I add three words to assist you in selecting appropriate music and song. They correspond to the musical, liturgical, and pastoral judgements referred to in *Music in Catholic Worship:*

Taste: Music used in worship should reflect a sensitivity to all the current cultural expressions of the assembly balanced with a counter-cultural resistance to our "throw-away" mentality which only values the new. It should assist in "handing on" the faith tradition by allowing young people to observe adults' appreciation for songs and melodies which unite us with the believers who have gone before us. Music should always direct us to experience and share the presence of God in our midst. Regardless of style, all liturgical music should be done well, with care, and with proper preparation. Involving and apprenticing young singers and instrumentalists is one way of developing their appreciation for the variety of musical styles appropriate for liturgy. (DMC #32)

Text: The language of musical expression should evoke the response of those gathered in glorifying God and giving thanks. Because song unites the voices of all those present, its power as an acclamation of the people should be given the greatest consideration. Those acclamations which are part of the liturgical rite should be sung whenever possible. Experience shows that people sing best when they do not sing everything, and tend to sing less when a choir is more predominant. Preference should be given for music which is performed live, but because of cultural conditioning, adolescents demonstrate a unique ability to appropriate recorded music as their own expression and will often "sing along" with great conviction. (DMC #32) Attention should be given to selecting music which corresponds with liturgical function: acclamation, responsorial, hymn, or reflection.

Tact: Sensitivity and respect for all present at worship is critical; this includes consideration of the one who will preside. Too frequently the needs of adolescents are tacked upon the pastor's door in "Wittenburg-ian" fashion as a set of demands to be met. The balance between tradition and innovation must be sensitive to the ability of groups or individuals to adapt to changes in the rites, recognizing that liturgy is not private devotion, yet must encourage the active participation of the faithful, including youth.

Here are five simple criteria for choosing songs for worship:
1. Does it say what we want to sing?
2. Will it help the whole assembly to pray?
3. Is this song singable by a large group? (range, repetition, melody)
4. Does the song fit this liturgical situation? (sound, style, rhythm)
5. Does the song fit the rest of our liturgical setting and plan?

Participation through Presence and Response

The image of adolescent males standing stoically silent while the assembly sings is one which disheartens and undermines those who prepare worship. Alternating desires to confront and ignore this seemingly non-participative behavior are cause for trying all sorts of things within liturgy. For whatever reasons some youth and some adults are not willing to sing. Creative energy directed toward getting them to sing might be better spent considering the other ways that individuals are joined with the assembly in praising and glorifying God. Do not underestimate their very presence, even though they may appear to be uninvolved.

Additionally, the *Directory* suggests that introductory remarks and other aspects of the gathering rites, use of silent prayer, and responses or involvement in the readings are also pathways to participation. (DMC #23, #37, and #47) When attempting to adapt eucharistic liturgy to young people's expressions, caution should be used in adding elements such as slide/music meditations, non-biblical readings, reflections or poems, or other responses which are not integral to the rites. Begin with an assumption that the rites are symbolically able to speak to the faith experience of youth, and try to creatively draw out that experience, rather than pre-determine it through other language or elements. An example of this approach might be designating ten minutes or so before the liturgy as quiet time, or an opportunity to share some of the events of the day or week which may be in the minds and hearts of those gathered. This session can be lead by someone who is skilled in drawing forth youth responses and therefore might complement, rather than contradict, the role of the presider as liturgy begins. A general rule of thumb is, do not encumber the rites needlessly.

Movement, Gesture, and Visuals.

Anything which can be done to unite body and soul, head and heart, will improve the worship experience for young people, particularly younger adolescents. We believe that Jesus was the Word made flesh, but our liturgies too frequently are words, words, and more words. We need to pay more attention to the symbols of our worship and the way in which they are visually engaging. In view of the psychology of young people, gestures, posture, and opportunities for movement within the rites will increase their sense of the community united in worshipping the Creator. (DMC #33, #34)

Visual elements and artwork can also be employed. A slide/music meditation, for example, might be effective in that time before liturgy I suggested above, as a way of setting the environment for worship, rather than attempting to be an interpretation of the Scriptures. (DMC #35) Movement from one part of the worship space to another is also a way of defining and uniting the different rites. For example, when using a church for small group Eucharist, gathering the assembly around the eucharistic table prior to the Eucharistic Prayer may be appropriate. Incorporating movement into other devotions such as the Stations of the Cross can also be powerful experiences for youth.

Ritual gestures with adolescents will require some pre-discussion of the significance of using our bodies in praise. Youth, are very body and appearance-conscious. Even such generally accepted practices, such as holding hands during the Our Father, can evoke more distractive behavior than prayerful response. Yet, I have found gesture incorporated into a sung response or as part of blessings or commissionings to be very well received and prayerful when preceded by a minimal explanation of its purpose. (DMC #54) Youth do not want to do something alone. Therefore, it helps to appeal to their unanimity and care for one another. Again, an overall caution is that movement, gestures, and visuals be integral rather than additional to the rites.

Environment and Hospitality.

Too often overlooked is the effect which environment and hospitality have upon the worship experience. I gave some suggestions for the physical space earlier and I have discussed the overall effect of a welcoming outreach to youth as having significant impact on their readiness for celebration. Here I would add a concern for not overwhelming young people with our love and care so as to smother their need to feel rebellious. When adults appropriate youth culture as their own it ceases to be youth culture. (Perhaps that's why fashions, fads, and musical styles keep changing!) Our attention should be given to helping adolescents feel accepted by the community in their uniqueness, good qualities and bad, in the image of a God who loves each one of us unconditionally.

But as adults—elders of the faith community—we must also take seriously our responsibility to help youth identify aspects of culture and social conditions which are not aligned in conscience with the Gospel. When Jesus met the woman at the well, he listened to her story and let her know of his care and concern for her, but he also challenged her lifestyle in true compassion for the struggle which she faced. We can follow no better an example than the Master's as we prepare to celebrate liturgy with young people. As Erik Erikson so aptly phrased, "In no other stage of the life cycle...are the promise of finding oneself and the threat of losing oneself so closely allied." (Erikson 244) Today's adolescents face crises and pressures particular to the signs of our times which are unimaginable to adults who grew up in earlier periods. As adults prepare for worship, we need to adopt an attitude of care and compassion for the struggles which youth face. Then we will become that Body of Christ made flesh in the events of their lives.

Liturgical Ministers.

The roles which youth may rightfully fulfill within liturgy are a frequent source of controversy, debate, and pastoral concern. These controversies range from whether or not girls can be altar servers to what are the "requirements" for being a eucharistic minister. The *Directory* states clearly that children (youths) are to perform a variety of liturgical roles as befits their experience and training for exercising those functions. (#22) It's not my intention here to try to untangle the above mentioned arguments. Rather, I would make several references to liturgical documents which I believe support a more inclusive than restrictive stance on these issues.

First, the command which Jesus gave the disciples at the Last Supper was to take, eat, drink and do these things as a way of commemorating his saving action in our lives. We remember, we celebrate, we believe. That is the foundation of our faith. Through baptism, we believe that each one of us is united to Christ and to each other as the community of believers, in the life, work and mission of the Church—the Body of Christ. *(Constitution on the Sacred Liturgy* #6 and #14) It's our right and responsibility to carry out that work and worship. Church laws which interpret that command of the Lord must first of all respect the universal intent of Jesus' action. When such laws "hinder" that commemoration, they stand in opposition to the sacramental nature of the Church, and to the individual sacraments as signs of Jesus' continuing saving action in our midst. (CSL #47 and #48)

Secondly, full participation in the liturgical celebration is the goal for all Christians by virtue of their baptism *(General Instruction to the Roman Missal,* #3) and everyone has the right and duty to take part according to the diversity of orders and functions. (GIRM #58)

Thirdly, the General Instruction goes on to place special emphasis on preparing individuals for these roles. (GIRM #65 - #73) This is reinforced in more recent documents which call for those who come forward to exercise the ministries to be of excellent character, and living a Christian life. *(Holy Communion* 13)

As I discussed earlier, the link between liturgy and catechesis suggests that young people be instructed in the content and form of liturgy, but we might add here that such catechesis should systematically prepare youth to assume their rightful place in the liturgical ministries. Again, I would highly recommend that an "apprenticing" approach be used whereby adults, one-on-one, serve as mentors to young persons who come forward for the ministerial roles of acolyte, lector, greeter, and eucharistic minister. The intergenerational nature of this approach reinforces the responsibility of the community to hand on the traditions of the faith to its young.

In cases where pastors or local dioceses have legislated against such opportunities for youth, I encourage you to return to the documents for a source of conviction, and in a spirit of Christian prayer and respect, request an interpretation of such laws in the light of Church teaching. If such an approach is unsuccessful in modifying practice, let your conscience be formed in light of Christ's teaching. Even in the most limited environments adequate opportunities exist for celebrating non-eucharistic liturgies during which youth may proclaim the Scriptures and assist their peers in prayer and worship. I will address the possibilities for non-eucharistic liturgies later in this chapter.

STEP FIVE: ASSIGNING RESPONSIBILITIES

The next phase of preparation is translating all the discussions and plans into action. Reserve the last ten to fifteen minutes of any liturgy preparation team meeting to assigning responsibilities and writing out what each person has agreed to accomplish prior to the liturgical event. Here's a simplified list of questions which may be of assistance:

1. Who's responsible for coordinating all aspects of this liturgy?
2. Who will contact the presider or homilist (in the case when that individual is not present for this meeting)?
3. Who will make arrangements for the use of the worship space, either scheduling or requesting necessary permissions?
4. Who is responsible for hospitality or other social activities surrounding the liturgy?
5. Who will request the necessary copyright permissions?
6. Who will prepare the Order of Worship (if one is being used)?
7. Who will coordinate the music or choir, or be a contact to the music director?
8. Who is responsible for stipends and other expenses?
9. Who will make plans for any needed announcements or publicity about the event?
10. When will we meet to evaluate the liturgical event?

When youth are involved in these preparations for the first time, make sure that they have the necessary information to carry out the tasks they are assigned. If numbers allow, designate two or more youth to work together on a task, perhaps pairing an older youth with one who is less experienced in these matters.

STEP SIX: CELEBRATION, THEN EVALUATION

Following the liturgical celebration in importance is the task of evaluating the experience for its pastoral success in leading the participants to a deeper understanding and expression of faith. Since liturgy is at the same time a communal and individual reality, answers to any evaluating question are likely to be varied. I would make three general suggestions regarding evaluation of liturgy:

First, let any liturgical celebration be evaluated in the light of time and the community's overall direction and sense of worship. (Not to make light of the metaphor, even restaurant critics review an establishment more than once before making their recommendations.) Young people especially need to be encouraged to reserve judgements on their individual liturgical experiences so as to consider them in the relationship to the total outreach of the community. An opposite caution is also recommended when youth have had a peak faith experience at a retreat or small group liturgy. In this instance, call their attention to the other dynamics which helped to make it such a powerful event for them.

Secondly, let norms and criteria be established by which you evaluate specific liturgical celebrations in light of generally held directives for how liturgy should take place in your community. The process by which your committee or team discerns those norms could be a prayerful and catechetical experience. Such norms and criteria serve as benchmarks by which progress in improving worship for youth may be observed.

Respecting the uniqueness of individual situations and pastoral needs, I choose not to articulate specific norms or criteria here. I suggest that the remarks I have made in my two essays serve as vehicles for determining the ideals your team may wish to hold up as values or objectives. I have tried to make references to the liturgical documents, and would further suggest them as another starting point. (Be sure to consult Chapter 7, "Qualities and Criteria for Liturgical Celebrations" for assistance in establishing norms and criteria.)[5]

Thirdly, establish a regular process which will be used for evaluating. I suggest three simple questions as a starting point:

1. In light of our own experience and our observation of others' experiences, what went well at this liturgy?
2. Given our best sense of what should happen at liturgy (norms and criteria), what might have been improved?
3. Knowing that liturgy is most successful when it is a part of our commitment to the Gospel, what suggestions can we make for future worship experiences?

There is a tendency to evaluate liturgy even while concluding the rites and packing things away. If we are convinced that the final criteria for liturgy is how we live the Christian life, then a certain distance of time will lend other insights to our immediate response to how things went. It might even be helpful to record the team's response following an event, and then later at the next preparation meeting. Above all, never lose sight of our belief that salvation is God's work. We are only human instruments of His grace. In our human nature, we will continue to be perfected in God's holy plan.

SUGGESTIONS FOR NON-EUCHARISTIC LITURGIES

Throughout my two essays many of my suggestions and comments have been directed toward eucharistic liturgies. Frequently parishes and schools have many more opportunities for non-eucharistic liturgical celebrations with youth. These occasions can provide youth ministers, and other adults, the chance to celebrate and pray with adolescents using the metaphors, music, and expressions which relate well to their lives and culture. I offer four general suggestions.

MORNING AND EVENING PRAYER: THE LITURGY OF THE HOURS

One of the reforms of the Second Vatican Council which has taken somewhat longer to be fully instituted is the opportunity for the laity to regularly recite the divine office. (CSL #100) As the official morning and evening prayer of the Church, Lauds and Vespers have a regular pattern and formula which should be followed when prayed with a large assembly. However, the structure of the Hours gives ample opportunity for creative use of psalms, songs, and responses which reflect the expressions of youth. Several contemporary composers have written settings of the common psalms, canticles, and responses which are available as recordings as well.

THE REVISED RITES OF RECONCILIATION

One of the most prayerful and powerful liturgical experiences I have had recently came as coordinator of liturgy for the Mid-America Youth Ministry Conference. The second night of the conference was to feature an address by Dr. Michael Warren which was to be followed by a reconciliation service. In our preparation, we had selected the Spanish hymn "Habre Mis Ojos, Senor" (Open My Eyes, Lord) to begin the service. Dr. Warren's address to the 900 youth and youth ministers present referred frequently to a textile wall-hanging behind the main podium which displayed the face of Christ in a fascinating mosaic style. As he concluded his talk, which challenged us to see the face of Christ in the world events, arm raised and pointing to the mosaic, the lights dimmed for liturgy and we began to sing, "Open my eyes, Lord, I want to see Jesus..." The Spirit had infused that moment with a sense of awe and grief, wonder and gratefulness for the loving forgiveness of our God.

Unfortunately, the power of the Rite of Reconciliation remains somewhat closed to the experience of many young people. Whether due to lack of adequate catechesis, positive experiences, or the generally uninformed image this sacrament has, youth ministers do young people a disservice by not providing more opportunities for its celebration. Adolescents are frequently wrestling with feelings of guilt, despair, hopelessness, anger, frustration, uncertainty and sorrow. The rites of reconciliation provide an occasion for the Church to minister sacramentally to their brokenness.

TRADITIONAL AND DEVOTIONAL PRAYER

The responsibility for handing on the traditions of our faith include sharing the devotional prayer which has been handed down to us by our parents and grandparents. Such expressions as the Rosary, Stations of the Cross, Novenas, and devotions to the saints are a way of uniting us with the Church throughout the ages.

These prayer forms are not likely to be ones that youth actively pursue, yet they provide a special opportunity for youth ministers to connect the generations of believers. When young people are present for these devotions, they show respect for older members of the community.

Recently, several youth ministers have found great success by creatively involving youth in preparing the Stations of the Cross during Lent, scriptural recitations of the Rosary, and Bible vigils. There are likely to be other possibilities in your own situation. You will not find a wealth of resources for celebrating devotions with youth. My recommendation is to observe the possibilities available in your parish and then bring youth and adults together to strategize the creative alternatives. The results could be surprising to both groups, as well as helpful in improving the images they have of one another.

CELEBRATING THE RITUAL MOMENTS IN THE LIVES OF YOUTH

One of the most accessible ways of catechizing youth for liturgy is to regularly highlight the ritual moments of their young lives. These special events might include:
* Passing from one grade to the next
* Graduation from junior high to high school (or from 8th grade)
* Graduation from high school
* Homecoming (usually celebrated in the fall)
* Semester Exams

Other moments or issues which might be the focus of liturgical prayer are:
* Jobs
* Parents
* Friends
* Cross-cultural experiences
* Experience of a suicide or other tragedy
* Drugs or alcohol abuse
* "Downer Celebrations" (This is a suggestion by Don Kimball for times to celebrate the presence of God in spite of all the ugly things happening in our lives.) (Kimball 131)

A simple, but standard format for any of these times might use the following general pattern: gather, listen, respond, go forth. It might look like this:

Gather. The first movement should be one of sharing stories and experiences related to the event or issue being liturgized. This could be accomplished through a storyteller, through personal sharing, through contemporary music and discussion, art, or other possibilities.

Listen. In a second movement the people gathered hear the Word of God as revealed through the Scriptures and contemporary revelation. Creative reading or dramatization could bring new life to familiar passages. Comments in reflection, silence, or even testimonials might add to this movement.

Respond. The third movement should involve response through prayer, song, action, gesture, or dance. Visuals and music are likely to be most effective.

Go Forth. True response is a commitment to Christian action and virtue. Blessings, commissionings, pledges, group hugs and other symbolic action are some suggested ways to move on from the experience.

SUMMARY

I have tried to provide a foundation for preparing and evaluating worship for youth. I believe there are three building blocks of the foundation:

First is attention to the developmental issues of adolescence, including their psychological readiness for ritual, and the ways that community worship may need to adapt in response to those dynamics.

The second is catechesis when understood as part of total community outreach to young people. Catechesis through and for liturgy which develops personal and communal prayer is one dimension of total youth ministry.

The third is establishing a systematic involvement of youth in preparing worship, and a regular way of preparing youth for liturgical ministries. This includes youth participation in parish prayer and worship committees and young people taking responsibility for peer-group worship experiences.

The cornerstone of the foundation is Jesus Christ whose life, death and resurrection calls us to a covenant of faith and a life of service to His Gospel. A ministry to youth finds its origin, direction and support in Jesus' own ministry. We give thanks and praise for God's love made flesh each day in our lives as we look forward to everlasting life.

END NOTES

[1] Austin Fleming, *Preparing for Liturgy: A Theology and Spirituality* (Washington, D.C.: Pastoral, 1985). Fleming's commentary speaks especially to those who would distinguish between "traditional" and "contemporary" liturgies and place other distinctions upon creativity. Particularly enriching are his spiritual reflections for liturgical ministers found near the end of this highly-approachable volume.

[2] In presenting much of the following material, I am presupposing the reader's minimal familiarity with the basic liturgical documents including *The Constitution on the Sacred Liturgy, General Instruction on the Roman Missal* (and its Appendix for the U.S. Dioceses), *Music in Catholic Worship*, and it's complementary statement *Liturgical Music Today*, and *Environment and Art in Catholic Worship*. All of the above mentioned documents can be found in a useful format in *The Liturgy Documents: A Parish Resource*, edited by Mary Ann Simcoe, (Chicago: Liturgy Training Publications, 1985). Helpful historical information and a short commentary on each document is also part of the resource. One need not be a liturgical scholar to benefit from a reading of these sourcebooks. Similarly, the reader is encouraged to be familiar with the following basic sources to youth ministry theory: *A Vision for Youth Ministry* (Washington, DC: United States Catholic Conference, 1976), *The Challenge of Adolescent Catechesis* (Washington, D.C.: The National Federation for Catholic

Youth Ministry, 1986), and *Sharing the Light of Faith: The National Catechetical Directory* (Washington, DC: United States Catholic Conference, 1979).

[3] Here I am paraphrasing Elizabeth McMahon Jeep in her article "Liturgy with Children: Basic Liturgical Principles" which appeared as part of an entire issue of *Pastoral Music* (Volume 12:2, December - January 1988) devoted to the *Directory.* The series was a recap of the first conference held regarding Children and Liturgy sponsored by the National Pastoral Musicians' Association the previous summer in Scranton, Pennsylvania.

[4] Frequently, when presenting the seven components of youth ministry to a parish council or similar group, the participants will comment that these components are integral to the whole mission of the Church and are universal in their application. Youth ministers may need to take the *Vision* paper from underneath the "bushel" so that its light may shine in parishes.

[5] A helpful resource for this process is: Yvonne Cass and Joanne Sanders, *Groundwork: Planning Liturgical Seasons* (Chicago: Liturgy Training Publications, 1982). Other resources which you may find helpful are: Gilbert Ostdiek, *Catechesis for Liturgy* (Washington, D.C.: The Pastoral Press, 1986): 38-45; Dennis C. Smolarski, SJ, *How Not to Say Mass* (New York: Paulist, 1985); Mark Searle, *Liturgy Made Simple* (Collegeville: Liturgical, 1981); Thomas Baker and Frank Ferrone, *Liturgy Committee Basics, A No-Nonsense Guide* (Washington, DC: Pastoral, 1985); and Gabe Huck, *Liturgy with Style and Grace* (Chicago: Liturgy Training Publications, 1984).

WORKS CITED

Bishop's Study Text 1: *Holy Communion.* Washington, D.C.: USCC, 1984.

The Challenge of Adolescent Catechesis. Washington, D.C.: The National Federation for Catholic Youth Ministry, 1986.

Directory for Masses with Children (DMC). *Roman Missal.* International Committee on English in the Liturgy, Inc, 1973. Published in *The Liturgy Documents.* Chicago: Liturgy Training Publications, 1980.

Erikson, Erik. *Identity: Youth in Crisis.* New York: Norton, 1968.

Fleming, Austin. *Preparing for Liturgy: A Theology and Spirituality.* Washington, D.C.: The Pastoral Press, 1985.

Funk, Virgil. "Blessed Be Jesus Whom You Sent to Be the Friend of Children and of the Poor." *Pastoral Music*, Volume 12:2, December - January 1988.

Kimball,Don. *Power and Presence: A Theology of Relationships.* San Francisco: Harper, 1987.

Nelson, John S. "Research on Adolescent Moral and Faith Development." *Readings in Youth Ministry—Volume I: Foundations.* Washington, D.C.: NFCYM, 1986.

Ostdiek, OFM. Gilbert. *Catechesis for Liturgy.* Washington, D.C.: Pastoral , 1986.

Philibert O.P., Paul. "Readiness for Ritual: Psychological Aspects of Maturity in Christian Celebration." *Alternative Futures for Worship: Volume I - General Introduction.* Edited by Regis A. Duffy, O.F.M. Collegeville: Liturgical , 1987.

Pope John Paul II. *Catechesi Tradendae.* Washington, D.C.: USCC, 1979.
Sharing the Light of Faith: The National Catechetical Directory. NCCB.
Washington, D.C.: USCC, 1979.
A Vision for Youth Ministry. USCC, Department of Education. Washington,
D.C.: USCC, 1976.

RESOURCES FOR LITURGICAL MUSIC

These are the four major producers and distributors of contemporary liturgical
music. There are others, but not as widely used and known. I certainly encourage
you to make use of good resources which may be available to your area.

G.I.A Publications, Inc, 7404 S. Mason Avenue, Chicago, IL 60638 (312) 496-
3800.
Artist/Resource: David Haas, James Moore, Marty Haugen, Michael Joncas,
Gather to Remember Hymnal, Taize Volumes, *Worship III Hymnal, Lead Me,
Guide Me Black Hymnal, Celebrate Hymnal.*
North American Liturgy Resources, 10801 N. 23rd Avenue, Phoenix, AZ
85029. (602) 864-1980
Artist/Resource: The Jesuits, The Dameans, Tim Manion, Rory Cooney,
Michael Joncas, Dan Consiglio, Tom Kendzia, Carey Landry, Grayson Warren
Brown, *Glory and Praise* Hymnals.
Oregon Catholic Press, P.O. Box 14809, Portland, OR 97214. (503) 231-2594.
Artist/Resource: Bernard Huijbers, Tom Conry, Bob Hurd, Jerry Goebel,
Breaking Bread Hymnals, *Thomas More Collections*, several Hispanic
Collections
J.S.Paluch Co./World Library, 3815 N. Willow Road, Schiller Park, IL 60176.
(312) 678-9300.
Artist/Resource: Jim Marchionda, *New People's Mass Book, We Celebrate
Missalette, Cantemos al Senor* Hymnal

Another source of music to use with youth is Contemporary Christian Music.
These artists reflect the diversity of secular musical styles which are currently
popular, from rock to country and everything in-between. Most of the well-known
artists are published by WORD, Inc. in Waco, Texas. You can listen to these tapes
at local Christian bookstores. Artists to consider are: Tom Franzak (a Catholic
artist), Amy Grant, Sandi Patti, Petra, John Michael Talbot, Michael Card. A good
resource for using popular music in prayer and liturgy is *Top Music Countdown*
and the other publications and media available from Cornerstone Media, published
by Tabor. Check them out for some great suggestions and information on
contemporary culture.

Chapter 7

Qualities and Criteria for Liturgical Celebrations

By Gilbert Ostdiek

What makes a liturgy a good liturgy? What qualities should we work for in our liturgy? By what criteria are we to judge whether or not a liturgy was pastorally successful? How does one go about establishing these qualities and criteria?

It comes as no surprise that liturgists and liturgy committee wrestling with these questions have come up with a variety of answers.[1] And perhaps that is as it should be, given what we have been saying here about the uniqueness of each pastoral situation in which the liturgy is celebrated. Selecting and prioritizing the qualities and criteria for liturgies that are appropriate to the community it serves is something each liturgy committee has to do for itself. The time and energy spent in establishing and implementing a working set of qualities and criteria might end up being one of the single most important things a liturgy committee can do. It forces us to go beyond a superficial, technician's approach to the liturgy and to address the deeper issue of what our pastoral goals are in preparing and evaluating liturgical celebrations.

My intent in this article is to provide working materials for that task rather than a ready-made formula. The materials will be of a general kind, with more particular suggestions to follow in part two, and will be summarized first from the liturgical documents and then from my own point of view. The materials will also seem massive. They are presented only as idea-starters. A committee will have to select a few as its priorities, perhaps starting with one or two at a time.

MINING THE OFFICIAL DOCUMENTS

There are three documents to which we can turn for help in our efforts to establish the qualities and criteria for a good liturgy. The first of these is Vatican II's *Constitution on the Sacred Liturgy*. Chapter one of the Constitution concludes with several sets of norms to be implemented in the liturgical revisions. These norms offer some helpful guidelines for our questions.

One such set of norms (CSL #26-32 [DOL #26-32]) identifies several qualities which are to characterize the new liturgy. The liturgy should be celebrated communally by an assembly, rather than in private. The assembly should be fully, consciously, and actively engaged in the celebration. The various liturgical roles should be distributed within the assembly and all members of the assembly should be allowed to exercise their proper roles without infringement.

Another group of norms (CSL #33-36 [DOL #33-36]) reaffirms a historic set of qualities that have been part of the genius of the Roman rite since ancient times. In a passage often quoted in answer to the question of what qualities to look for in a liturgy, the constitution says: "The rites should be marked by a noble simplicity; they should be short, clear, and unencumbered by useless repetitions; they should be within the people's powers of comprehension and as a rule not require much explanation". (CSL #34 [DOL #34])

A final set of norms (CSL #37-40 [DOL #37-40]) calls the Church to both preserve the substantial unity of the Roman rite and adapt it to the local cultures of people.

The second document which furnishes us with useful material is the U.S. bishops' *Music in Catholic Worship*, cited earlier. The third section of that document (MCW #23-41) outlines three judgments which are to guide planners in selecting music for a celebration. The musical judgment asks whether the piece is good musical art. The liturgical judgment asks whether that piece can also serve the liturgy, since good art does not automatically make good liturgical art. The pastoral judgment asks whether that which is good liturgical music in itself suits the particular assembly and occasion for which it will be used. The committee must be able to answer all three questions in the affirmative. These three judgments could easily be made to serve as criteria for every symbolic form used in the liturgy.

The final document which has much to offer toward our discussion is another one issued by the U.S. bishops, *Environment and Art in Catholic Worship*. Its first section on the requirements of worship (EACW #9-26) is particularly helpful. The bishops write that the liturgy should be traditional, yet contemporary; it should express both human hospitality and the mystery of God; it should be a personal-communal experience. They call for a manner of celebrating which opens up our symbols. Art forms, they say, are to serve the liturgy and should be marked by quality and appropriateness.

Together these documents offer a wealth of ideas from which we can draw in setting down our lists of qualities and criteria. They deserve our careful and thoughtful reading.

MAPPING THE QUALITIES AND CRITERIA

How can we pull together in manageable form what these and similar documents, as well as our growing experience, teach us about what to look for as we prepare and evaluate liturgy? It may be of help to organize them using a three-fold schema employed by anthropologists studying rituals: the performers of the ritual, the structure of the ritual, and the ritual symbols and actions. I offer this schematization as a second set of working materials to help sort through the question of qualities an criteria. The materials are purposely very detailed in order to stir ideas; an actual working list would contain no more than a few qualities and criteria, chosen as priorities because of their particular importance for our assemblies.

A word about the layout. Each section of the schema begins with a basic norm. The qualities to prepare for and evaluate in a good liturgy are then given in italics with a brief explanation. Finally, evaluation questions are interspersed for each quality, and summary questions attempt to focus larger areas of concern. These questions could be easily recast for use in preparing as well. References to documents are included for those who wish to study the sources further.

PERFORMERS OF THE LITURGY

THE ASSEMBLY

Norm: Communal celebration of the liturgy is the norm. The primary criterion of good liturgy is the full, active, conscious participation of the assembly. (CSL #14 [DOL #14])[2]

Prepare and evaluate:

1. *Full Participation*: Ministers who see the liturgy as their personal action and, however graciously or grudgingly, allow the assembly to assist do not observe this norm. Full participation means that the assembly not only takes an active part, but that the liturgy is truly theirs. It also means that those who prepare the liturgy are to consult the assembly and adapt the celebration to their culture, circumstances, and spiritual needs. Evaluation question: Was the liturgy truly the assembly's action?

2. *Active participation*: The active participation called for by Vatican II is not merely external activity, but a participation that engages the mind and spirit by engaging the body and its senses. Were members of the assembly fully and actively engaged in body and spirit?

3. *Conscious participation*: To use an alternate phrasing of Vatican II, this means that the assembled people are to take part in the liturgy "fully aware of what they are doing." There are two levels to this awareness. First, people are to be fully aware of doing the liturgy. They are entitled to adequate instruction and preparation beforehand and to restrained, unobtrusive explanations and participation aids during the liturgy so that they can understand and follow the rites. Second, and more importantly, they are to be fully aware of doing the liturgy as God's people. The celebration should enable the people, gathered to hear God's word and to renew covenant, to sense God's presence and workings in their lives, to know themselves as God's people and followers of Jesus Christ, called to witness and spread the kingdom through their lives. Did the assembly take part fully aware of what they were doing?

Summary question: Did the assembly hear the word of God, pray, and offer praise?

THE MINISTERS

Norm: "In liturgical celebrations each one, minister or layperson, who has an office to perform, should do all of, but only, those parts which pertain to that office by the nature of the rite and the principles of liturgy" . (CSL #28 [DOL #28])[3]

Prepare and evaluate:

4. *Variety of roles*: Well-ordered liturgy requires that various roles be filled by ordained ministers, special ministers, and members of the assembly. Were the various liturgical roles distributed and respected?

5. *Adequate preparation*: Those who exercise liturgical ministries are to be "trained to perform their functions in a correct and orderly manner" (CSL #29 [DOL #29]) and informed of their responsibilities beforehand "so that nothing is improvised". (GIRM #313 [DOL #1703]) Were the ministers prepared?

6. *Effective performance*: Effective liturgy depends on the human naturalness, the respectful care, and the prayerfulness of those who minister. Did the ministers perform their roles effectively?

Summary Question: Did the ministers serve the assembly?

STRUCTURE OF THE LITURGY

THE OVERALL PATTERN

Norm: The integrity of a liturgical celebration requires that it preserve the substantial unity of the Roman rite while allowing for legitimate variations and adaptations to different groups, regions, and peoples, and that the harmonious interconnections of its parts be maintained (CSL #37-38, 50, [DOL #37-38, 50]; GIRM #8 [DOL #1398]).

Prepare and evaluate:

7. *Integrity of structure*: Was the liturgy celebrated with fidelity to the structure of the Roman rite and to the culture and spiritual needs of the assembly?

8. *Proper value given each part*: Not all parts of a liturgy are of equal importance. For example, in the Mass the introductory and concluding rites are of secondary importance compared to the liturgy of the Word and the liturgy of the Eucharist. (MCW #43) Was the relative importance of each part respected?

9. *Rhythm and balance*: Effective liturgy is marked by rhythm, balance, and movement between the parts, so that the assembly experiences moments of intensity and relaxation and a buildup to properly chosen peaks, such as the Gospel, great amen, and communion, as it moves through the rite. Was there proper rhythm, balance, and movement between the various parts?

Summary Question: Did the liturgy catch the people up in its flow - gathering them, feeding them on God's word, uncovering the experience of dying and rising with Christ at the core of their daily lives, and sending them forth renewed?

THE COMPONENT PARTS

Norm: The integrity of a liturgical celebration requires that it respect the intrinsic nature and pastoral purpose of each part (CSL #50 [DOL #50]; GIRM #24-57 [DOL #1414-1447]; MCW #42-49) while making judicious use of the variations and alternatives provided in the rite for the spiritual good of the assembly.[4]

Prepare and Evaluate:

10. *Integrity of each part*: Integrity is less a matter of doing a literal rendition of rubric and text than it is of fulfilling the intrinsic nature and pastoral purpose of

each part. For example, the *Directory for Masses with Children* (#24 [DOL #2157]) provides that another adult may be allowed to give the homily if the presider finds it difficult to adapt himself to the mentality of the children, on the principles that it is of greater pastoral importance that the Word by preached effectively to the children than that the normal regulations regarding homilies be observed. That directory contains many similar examples. Were each of the component parts (gathering, Word, sacraments, sending) celebrated with fidelity to the Roman rite and to the culture and the spiritual needs of the assembly?

11. *Proper value of each element*: Not every element within a given part of the liturgy is of equal importance. For example, the primary elements of the preparation rite are the bringing of the gifts, the placing of them on the altar, and the prayer over the gifts. All other elements are the ones we should plan to enhance with song and special ritual care. Was the relative importance of each element respected?

12. *Pastoral adaptations and variations*: Variations and alternate ways of doing the rite (for example, the alternate readings, prayers, and presidential introductions provided in the various parts of the rite) are there to be used. Was there responsible and effective pastoral use of the variety of options?

Summary Question: Did each part of the liturgy serve its pastoral purpose?

SYMBOLIC LANGUAGES AND SYMBOLS OF THE LITURGY

THE MANY SYMBOLIC LANGUAGES AND SYMBOLS

Norm: Just as the human reality of Jesus mediates God's presence to us, so too our bodily actions and use of human objects in the liturgy tangibly express and bring about God's sanctifying presence to us and our worship of God in spirit and truth. Liturgical celebration depends radically on the honest use of the full range of symbolic languages and liturgical symbols. These "signs perceptible to the human senses" either nourish or destroy faith by the way in which they are performed. Full participation thus involves both the spirit and the body in all its sense. (CSL #7 [DOL #7]; GIRM #5 [DOL #1395]; MCW #1-9; EACW #13)

Prepare and evaluate:

13. *Variety of symbols, symbolic languages*: Each liturgical language or symbol, such as silence, posture, ritual gesture, song, and season communicates the mystery of God's presence in its own unique way. No one of them should be reduced to being a mere illustration for another of the languages, such as the spoken word; each should be allowed to speak in its own way. Were the various liturgical symbols and symbolic languages used fully, with respect for their uniqueness?

14. *Balance and harmony*: Ritual communication in liturgy, as in all cases of human interaction, shows an interplay and redundancy between the various languages being used. Were the liturgical symbols and languages balanced and in harmony in what they said to the assembly?

15. *Full embodiment*: Ritual communication in liturgy, like all human ritual communication, is based on bodily interaction and makes use of all the senses, especially touch, sight, and hearing. A liturgy which treats us as disembodied

spirits denies our wholeness. Was the liturgy fully embodied, especially by the liturgical ministers?

Summary Question: Did the liturgical symbols and languages together speak to and for the assembly, nourishing their faith and lives?

THE ARTISTIC QUALITY

Norm: Every liturgical symbol or ritual action must have an artistic quality. Liturgy takes its inspiration for symbol and ritual action from the fine arts, both visual arts and performing arts, and welcomes the artistic expressions, both folk and classic, of past ages and of contemporary peoples, when they are able to serve the liturgy beautifully and worthily. (CSL #122-124 [DOL #122-124]; GIRM #253-254 [DOL #1643-1644]; EACW #18)

Prepare and evaluate:

16. *Simple and attractive beauty of objects*: Liturgical objects are to possess a quality that bespeaks both an honesty and genuineness of materials and the artist's care and gift in crafting them with a special touch. (EACW #12, 20) Did the liturgical symbols possess a simple and attractive beauty and show the artist's hand?

17. *Noble simplicity of rites*: In design, "the rites should be marked by a noble simplicity; they should be short, clear, and unencumbered by useless repetitions; they should be within the people's powers of comprehension and as a rule not require much explanation". (CSL #34 [DOL #34]; EACW #17) Did the celebration possess a noble simplicity?

18. *Effective performance/use*: In the liturgy ritual actions should be performed and liturgical objects used in a way that is humanly attractive, natural, and invitational, and with a care and attentiveness that makes the ritual moment special. (MCW #7, 9, 21; EACW #11-12) Were ritual actions performed and liturgical objects used effectively?

THE LITURGICAL QUALITY

Norm: Every ritual action or symbolic object used in the liturgy must be appropriate to the liturgy, possessing a transparency that invites the assembly to experience its God and itself as God's people. (EACW #21-22, 12)

Prepare and Evaluate:

19. *Liturgical appropriateness*: "The work of art must be appropriate in two ways: 1) it must be capable of bearing the weight of mystery, awe, reverence, and wonder which the liturgical action expresses; 2) it must clearly serve (and not interrupt) ritual action which has its own structure, rhythm and movement". (EACW #21; also #22, 25) Were the symbolic objects and ritual actions appropriate to the liturgy?

20. *Multivocal symbols and ritual expressions*: Symbols and symbolic actions are, by nature, capable of bearing many meanings. Liturgical symbols should not be excessively restricted, especially by explanatory words, in what they can mean for the assembly. Were the multiple meanings of the symbols and symbolic actions respected?

21. *Fidelity to tradition and contemporary culture*: Liturgical symbols and symbolic actions are to speak in a tongue ever ancient and ever new. Were they faithful to tradition and to contemporary cultural expressions of the assembly?

Summary Question: Did the liturgical symbols and actions serve the people and invite them to experience the unspeakable mystery of God?

THE PASTORAL QUALITY

Norm: The spiritual good of the assembled people is the final pastoral criterion for all effective planning and celebration of the liturgy. (GIRM #313 [DOL #1703])

Prepare and Evaluate:

22. *Effective vehicles of communication*: Since liturgical symbols and ritual languages are all "vehicles of communication", (MCW #7) it is impossible for them not to convey something to the assembly. "Good celebrations foster and nourish faith. Poor celebrations may weaken and destroy it". (MCW #6) What did the celebration communicate to the assembled people?

23. *Opening up of symbols*: The renewed liturgy "requires the opening up of our symbols, especially the fundamental ones of bread and wine, water, oil, the laying on of hands, until we can experience all of them as authentic and appreciate their symbolic value". (EACW #15) Were the liturgical actions and symbols opened up to the assembly?

24. *Fidelity to the assembly*: The pastoral effectiveness of a liturgy depends on the degree to which the liturgy is adapted to the culture, way of life, circumstances, and religious development of the people actually assembled to celebrate it. Was the celebration faithful to their spiritual needs?

Summary Question: "People in love make signs of love"; (MCW #4) did the celebration enable those present to express their love for God and each other?

SELECTING QUALITIES AND CRITERIA

A wide, detailed array of qualities and criteria have been purposely presented in the above outline to serve as idea-starters for us. It is obvious we cannot work on all these qualities and criteria at the same time in preparing and evaluating liturgy. A selection has to be made for our individual pastoral situations. The few remarks which follow are offered as a help to guide us in that selection.

First, as the summary evaluation questions have tried to insist, our primary pastoral concern must always be to care for God's people at prayer. Their full and active participation must be the primary norm we follow in preparing and evaluating the celebration, their spiritual good must be the final goal of all our caring for their prayer.

Second, we need to develop a set of priorities which enfleshes that orientation to the assembly. We might, for example, make our own the three factors, listed earlier, which seem critical in enabling the assembly to feel at home in the celebration and to worship and pray. One is fidelity to the assembly, both its liturgical tradition and the spiritual needs and life-situation of its members, a fidelity which tells us that the celebration is truly "ours." Another is the reverent care with which the central liturgical actions and symbols are prepared and performed/used, a care which tells us that what we do is a holy sacrament. A third is the obvious, contagious prayerfulness of those assembled, especially the ministers.

Third, we need to start small, selecting a few qualities and criteria to guide our preparation and evaluation in manageable ways. Thus, we might focus, one by one, on central ministerial actions which call for a congregational response, such as the reading of Scriptures, the musical exchanges within the assembly, or the breaking and distribution of the Eucharistic bread. Or again, we might take major feasts and seasons as an opportunity to attend to how we are using music and environment to heighten the assembly's sense of festivity. We might follow the example of one parish which has taken the qualities of hospitality and prayerfulness as the criteria on which celebrations are evaluated.

A final, sobering reminder is called for, lest we harbor impossible expectations about what we are to accomplish in caring for the people at prayer. In the end, all we can do is provide an atmosphere and an invitation to prayer and praise. The results depend on God's grace and each one's response. We cannot produce the inner prayer and praise on command.

SUMMARY

1. Both preparing and evaluating celebrations depend on an awareness of what makes a liturgy pastorally effective for the assembly. A working set of qualities and criteria can be gleaned from the Church's documents on liturgy which have shaped our experience of the renewed liturgy.

2. A detailed study outline of those qualities and criteria form the perspective of the performers, structures, and ritual symbols of the liturgy can stir our own ideas and help us reflect more carefully on the qualities we seek in a liturgy that is pastorally effective for our people.

3. In selecting the qualities and criteria we wish to stress, we should start small, set our priorities, and keep the full, active, and conscious participation of each particular assembly as our primary norm and their spiritual good as our ultimate pastoral goal.

END NOTES

[1] The few resources available on evaluation are relatively brief. See, for example: Leonel L. Mitchell, *Liturgical Change. How Much Do We Need?* (New York: Seabury, 1975): 16-21.

[2] See also: CSL #11, 19, 26-27, 30 (DOL #11, 19, 26-27, 30); GIRM #1-6 (DOL #1391-1396); MCW #15-18; EACW #27-38.

[3] See also: CSL #29, 58 (DOL #29, 58); GIRM #59-61, 65-73 (DOL #1449-1451, 1455-1463); MCW #10-14, 21-22, 33-38; EACW #37.

[4] See also: Sacred Congregation of Rites, *Musician Sacram* #11 (DOL #4132).

Chapter 8

Aids for Preparing Liturgical Celebrations

A. Guidelines for Reading Scripture

By Kathleen Fischer

Our concern in approaching Scripture in a new way is to take seriously the creative power of language and form. We want to live the biblical story so that it becomes our own story. Only then can the biblical word produce the same saving effect which it created in Israel and the early Church. To hear the Bible in this way we must learn to listen attentively. Elie Wiesel in *Souls on Fire* describes how his grandfather taught him that "to listen is to receive." We do not force the text to submit to us; we receive it. Wiesel listened intently to his grandfather's Hasidic tales, and so was carried into a universe "where facts became subservient to imagination and beauty." *(Souls on Fire* 6-7)

We come to a biblical passage with contemplative openness to its word, and with awareness of the personal questions and concerns that have brought us there. In this spirit we (1) attend carefully to the text itself, (2) call on historical and literary criticism for assistance, and (3) celebrate and live the text within a community of faith. Let us explore each of these steps more closely.

1. ATTEND CAREFULLY TO THE TEXT ITSELF

This may seem like strange advice. However, many Christians are afraid to trust their reading of a biblical text. We are aware that between us and the text stands the vast amount of learning that scholars have accumulated on the Bible over the years. We fear that we do not know enough to understand the Bible itself, so we turn first to a commentary or a theology book to help us find our way through it. Or our problem may be that a passage like Jesus' calming of the storm or the wedding feast at Cana seems all too familiar. It is so familiar, in fact, that we merely glance at it and assume that we know what it says.

However, the text is a locus of revelation. As revelation, it is not simply information; it is a relationship in which we are called to participate. We enter into a dialogue with the text, bringing our questions to it and allowing the biblical questions to address us: "Whom do you seek?" "Do you love me?" "Who do you say that I am?" The literary forms of the Bible can draw us into such a dialogue, since they are personal and searching. They can have this power, though, only if we really attend to the text and hear what is taking place in it.

One help in reading the text is to think of it as woven of many threads, like a tapestry on a loom. These threads or elements that make up the texture of a biblical passage are the character, their actions and interactions, the oppositions and contradictions that are woven into the text, and the beginning and ending which hold the passage together. An example will help to show how attention to the interrelated patterns and images within a biblical passage enables us to hear it in a fresh way and brings its power to life for us again.

The story of Jesus' meeting with Zacchaeus in Luke 19:1-10 needs to be read and reread attentively if we are to notice its detail and richness.[1] The two principal characters in the story are Jesus and Zacchaeus. In the first part of the story, this prophet who travels through Palestine teaching and healing is simply called "Jesus." He draws large crowds and attracts Zacchaeus' attention. Then something we may not have noted before occurs in the second part of the story: there is a change of names. In verses 7-10 this man Jesus is called "Lord" and "Son of Man," names of superior importance, suggesting divine titles. This change ties together the beginning and ending of the story. In verse 3 we are told that Zacchaeus "was anxious to see what kind of man Jesus was." He discovers that Jesus is Lord.

The passage presents the second character, Zacchaeus, to us in detailed fashion. Zacchaeus is rich, but his riches may not always have been acquired honestly, for he is called a sinner (v. 7) and Zacchaeus himself wonders "if I have cheated anybody"(v. 8). He is also a searcher, who cannot find what he is looking for: "He was anxious to see what kind of man Jesus was, but was too short and could not see him."(v. 3). At the end of the story this searching is transformed: "salvation has come"(v. 9); "the Son of Man has come to seek out and save" (v. 10). Zacchaeus was looking but could not find; Jesus comes to save and brings salvation. The story also shows the transformations which take place in the actions of Zacchaeus through this experience. In the beginning he is one who takes in, who gathers taxes. At the end of the story he shares and gives to others. He welcomes Jesus into his home (v. 6) and gives his goods to the poor (v. 8).

As we hear the details of this story, it reaches out to involve us. Zacchaeus finds joy in giving up his previous actions. He finds the Lord in Jesus, and this involves a transformation of his life. We, too, are searching to find out who Jesus is. And we are also sinners in need of forgiveness. We bring to the passage many questions about Jesus, and about our own lives. In the story of Zacchaeus we see that our search may transform not only our initial questions, but our very way of life. The story challenges us to be changed by the discovery of Jesus, to face our own need for repentance. In addition, it creates a yearning for the joy Zacchaeus found in such a change. The horizon of the biblical text fuses with our own horizon, giving us a deeper understanding of what salvation means.

As we become more familiar with a particular book of the Bible, it is also helpful to read biblical passages in light of the whole book. For example, we read the story of Zacchaeus with care not only when we read the questions within the story, but also when we hear in it echoes of Luke's other narratives and sayings. This individual story reflects Luke's major concerns and themes: Jesus as Savior bringing universal salvation, Jesus' care for the poor and outcasts, his compassion and mercy, and his gift of messianic joy. The story of Zacchaeus expresses these themes of Luke's Gospel in summary form. Therefore, reading this passage in light of the whole Gospel provides a constant interplay between text and context.

The Books of Ruth, Genesis, and the Song of Songs provide further illustrations of this kind of reading. Opening the pages of the Book of Ruth, we may be struck first by Ruth's fidelity to her mother-in-law, captured in the familiar refrain of 1:16-17: "Wherever you go, I will go; wherever you live, I will live." The book is the story of Ruth, a Moabite woman who, after the death of her husband, refuses to leave her mother-in-law, Naomi. They travel together to Bethlehem, where Ruth weds Boaz, a relative of her husband, and gives birth to Obed, the grandfather of David.

Reading the Book of Ruth as if it were revelation for us in symbolic form, we feel its invitation to enter into the rhythm of emptiness and fullness which occurs not only in our relationship to the earth, but on the widest personal and social levels as well. (Rauber 27-37) The opening verse of the book sounds this theme: "famine came to the land." This emptiness of the land is the setting for the loneliness of the widow which is described in verse 3: "Elimelech, Naomi's husband, died and she and her two sons were left." Naomi's two sons, one of them Ruth's husband Chilion, also die. The force of emptiness is further felt in the contrast between the barrenness of an old woman and the fullness of bearing children in verses 11-13: "And Naomi said, 'You must return, my daughters; why come with me? Have I any more sons in my womb to make husbands for you? Return, my daughters; go, for I am too old now to marry again.'" These images of famine, loneliness, and barrenness bring to life our personal experiences of anguish and loss and our own feelings of uselessness and despair.

Over against this deepening sense of emptiness, the story introduces the symbol of plenty: Naomi and Ruth return to Bethlehem "at the beginning of the barley harvest" (v. 22). This harvest image is the beginning of a movement of healing and the foreshadowing of a solution to Naomi's and Ruth's problems. The gathering harvest is the central image in the second part of the book.

> Everything culminates and merges in this image of ingathering: the wings of the Lord sweeping in to himself the people, the arms of Boaz gathering in to himself the maiden Ruth, the arms of the young men drawing into the barns the grain. It is a moment of imaginative splendor and depth. (Rauber 33)

The transformation that occurs between the beginning and the ending of the story is captured in the contrast between the book's images of famine and harvest. Emptiness and fullness are pervasive human experiences; on this level the book touches deep chords in us. We remember times when our own longing and darkness have issued in a harvest of comfort, peace, or new understanding. We recall seasons of thanksgiving, and unexpected joys, experiences of the goodness of God, and the fullness of God's love. The story unveils for us the presence of grace in the midst of ordinary human activities, and of life coming out of death. This is what its symbols reveal. They invite us to find God in the seasons of our lives.

Attentiveness to the artistic qualities of a text also rewards our reading of an ancient and familiar narrative, the saga of Abraham's sacrifice of Isaac in Genesis 22:1-19.[2] The austere beauty of this story demands disciplined attention to its language and imagery. We wonder as we approach the text: What does Abraham feel? What is he thinking? The author does not give us a minute description of Abraham's emotional state in face of what seems a monstrous command. To understand his feelings we must read carefully in verse 6 how Abraham carries the fire and knife in his own hands and gives the wood to Isaac so that his son will not be exposed to any harm. Then, as Abraham and Isaac approach the place of sacrifice, the narrative tempo slows. Through this slower pace and the build-up of verbs, we sense the tensions within Abraham.

> When they arrived at the place God had pointed out to him, Abraham built an altar there, and arranged the wood. Then he bound his son Isaac and put him on the altar on top of the wood. Abraham stretched out his hand and seized the knife to kill his son. (vv. 9-10)

The language is at once more exact and more hesitant. The arresting simplicity of these sentences is fraught with the depth and complexity of Abraham's decision.

The characters of Abraham and Isaac and their relationship to God are also revealed through the skillful use of dialogue. In the dialogue which opens the story we hear God's call and command, and Abraham's readiness to respond. In the description of Isaac there are also echoes of the larger story surrounding this narrative. The history and destiny of many are centered in this one child. Abraham had no heir and was given a child after long years of waiting.

> It happened some time later that God put Abraham to the test. 'Abraham, Abraham,' he called. 'Here I am,' he replied. 'Take your son,' God said, 'your only child Isaac, whom you love, and go to the land of Moriah. There you shall offer him as a burnt offering, on a mountain I will point out to you' (vv. 1-2).

Isaac is the child of promise, the future of Israel. Will God abandon the promise? This opening dialogue generates a tension between the divine plan and its ostensible failure to be fulfilled. The tension will be released only as the story's conclusion makes clear that what God wants is faith and trust, not human sacrifices. The story fuses literary art and theological vision, showing us by almost wordless restraint Abraham as paradigm of obedience and the steadfastness of God's promise.

As we are drawn into this narrative we begin to experience it as a revelation for us. We see the story of Abraham and Isaac as our story. Are we Isaac? Are we Abraham? Elie Wiesel calls it a story of fear, faith, defiance and laughter. "Why," he asks, "was the most tragic of our ancestors named Isaac, a name which evokes and signifies laughter? Here is why. As the first survivor, he had to teach us, the future survivors of Jewish history, that it is possible to suffer and despair an entire lifetime and still not give up the art of laughter." *(Messengers of God* 86) Through the symbolic disclosure that occurs in this biblical narrative, we see that God can lead his people into darkness, but that he also changes suffering into blessing. We understand what it means to be called and guided by God, and we see that God's promises endure in spite of all apparent failures. What is more, these truths are not abstract convictions for us. Through the narrator's skill, such revelation becomes personal and comprehensible. It takes a powerful and enduring hold on our imagination.

We have been listening to the Books of Ruth and Genesis to see how an artistic reading of the texts of Scripture can open us to the power of their themes and images. Attentiveness to image and metaphor is even more crucial in reading the poetry of Scriptures. The Song of Songs, for example, is a cluster of metaphors and images: wine, perfume, oil, sun, vineyards, flocks, earrings, necklaces, myrrh, henna flowers, turtledoves, pomegranates, honeycomb. Through these sensuous images we are invited to delight in the joy of human love. Themes of absence and presence, of losing and finding, are interwoven with these to point up the striving toward union between man and woman:

> On my bed, at night, I sought him whom my heart loves. I sought but did not find him. So I will rise and go through the City; in the streets and the squares I will seek him whom my heart loves...I sought but did not find him. The watchman came upon me on their rounds in the City: 'Have you seen him whom my heart loves?' Scarcely had I passed them than I found him whom my heart loves. I held him fast, nor would I let him go till I had brought him into my mother's house, into the room of her who conceived me. (3:1-4)

The meaning of the poem comes through its images and they are powerful communicators of emotion, of what it feels like to be lovers. These images convey a vision of the sexes as equal, of a situation where the woman as well as the man takes the initiative. The Song of Songs' images also invite comparison with the poetry of the first chapters of Genesis: the garden, the themes of paradise, man, woman, nature, and the tensions of union and separation. Paradise is lost in Genesis. In the Song of Songs, we see that paradise survives in the world through love, and is rediscovered through love. (Landy 513-528)

Images are associative and relational and operate on many levels of meaning. Their power can be seen, for example, in the poetry of the prophet Jeremiah. A key image in Jeremiah is that of water, in contrast to dryness. He complains to God:

> Why is my suffering continual, my wound incurable, refusing to be healed? Do you mean to be for me a deceptive stream with inconsistent water? (15:18)

Jeremiah distinguishes between God as the "fountain of living water" and those broken cisterns which allow the water to seep away. In another contrast, he speaks of the desert shrub and the tree planted "by the waterside." At the end of his drought poem in 14:1-17:13, Jeremiah refers to those who forsake God and turn away from him. Their names will be written in the dust because "they have abandoned the fountain of living water"(17:13). By means of these contrasting images Jeremiah calls us to a deep inner conversion. We are to realize that apart from God, all is drought and dust.

Jeremiah's images of water and drought show us that an image contains many layers of meaning. Because of this power of the imagination to connect and relate, to "free associate," reading the Bible in terms of its images and patterns often sets in motion a process of remembering. Just as the image of the garden in the Song of Songs calls up the garden of Genesis, so the image of the stranger in the Book of Ruth reminds us of a familiar theme in the Hebrew Scriptures:

> You must not molest the stranger and oppress him, for you lived as stranger in the land of Egypt (Ex 22:21)

Each use of the image of stranger is deepened by these wider associations. Likewise, the image of water found in Jeremiah's poetry takes on new meaning through its many biblical echoes. Water is, for example, the dominating image in the poetry of Psalm 42. Here the image is used both as the water of life and the water of death: "My soul thirsts for God, the God of life" (42:2); "Deep is calling to deep as your cataracts roar; all your waves, your breakers have rolled over me" (42:7). The images ultimately initiate that process of analogy whereby we see similarities and contrasts with our own experience, and this is their main function. For this reason Hans-Georg Gadamer calls the Bible a classic. For Gadamer, a classic is "that which speaks in such a way that it is not a statement about what is past, a mere testimony to something that still needs to be interpreted, but says something to the present as if it were said specially to it" (Gadamer 257). Continued reading of the Bible lets God's revelation illumine the enigmas of our lives. Our reading always remains unfinished. We can return continually to the biblical texts as new sources of understanding and love.

This power of the text depends on our deepening insight into its meaning. We reach the deeper significance. That is the way all symbols function. This fact underscores the importance of our second guide for reading Scripture.

2. CALL ON HISTORICAL AND LITERARY CRITICISM FOR ASSISTANCE

In our attentive listening to a text, the tools of historical and literary criticism can be of great help. There may be terms and customs which are not familiar to us. In the Zacchaeus passage, for example, it is helpful to understand the role of Jewish tax collectors in the first century and their alignment with foreign oppression. It is useful to know how high a sycamore tree is and whether you can see through its branches. In reading the book of Ruth, it is likewise helpful to know the status of the Moabites as foreigners in Israel's eyes, and the laws which give the poor the right to some of the gleanings of a harvest. We do need historical background. Its purpose, however, is to assist us in understanding the text. It never becomes primary. Astute literary criticism likewise serves a useful function. It can unlock the themes and images of a book and help us recognize the deeper structures in the text. But none of this substitutes for the encounter with the text itself.

Knowledge and study guide our reading of the Bible in another way. They help us deal with two concerns we have about approaching Scripture directly. The first is a fear of fundamentalism. We may be afraid that reading the text of the Bible itself will result in taking it too literally. However, imagination prevents such a literal reading; it is precisely what fundamentalism lacks. Asking of a biblical book like Revelation questions about the exact date and time of Jesus' coming results in a flattening of the book's imagery and poetry. Imagination is opposed to such a leveling of the richness of reality. Attention to the literary qualities of a text, rather than resulting in too literal a reading, leads to the recognition that truth is not simple, but complex. Further, we realize that there is more than one kind of truth. In addition to the truth of history and factual truth, there is the truth of myth, story, poetry, and proverb. This kind of truth is opposed to fundamentalism's tendency toward indoctrination and judgment. Truth conveyed in such forms as symbol and narrative is an invitation to respond in freedom. We are asked to enter sympathetically into the scene or symbol, to identify ourselves, for example, with actors who often display frailty, uncertainty, and sinfulness. Only such imaginative participation permits us to break out of judgement categories.

In addition to a fear of taking texts too literally, we may be afraid that if we approach biblical passages directly we will miss *the* message of the text. We want to know what the message of a book is. What is *the* truth which a certain passage teaches? We fear subjectivism. However, a passage may not teach one simple and single truth. Our reading may suggest several possible meanings of a passage, each of which is supported by the text itself. Paul Ricoeur speaks of this as a "surplus of meaning." An exact and literal meaning evades us because the text is overflowing. This is an indication of the richness of the biblical message. But to say that a text or image allows for many meanings is not to say that we are allowed to read anything at all into it. A text may permit a plurality of meanings, but it has its own laws which forbid other readings. As Paul Ricoeur has said:

> If it is true that there is always more than one way of construing a text, it is not true that all interpretations are equal. The text presents a limited field of possible constructions. (Ricoeur 79)

A text does not mean anything we might like it to mean. Part of the validation of its meanings come from the interaction of the threads of its tapestry, the characters, themes, images, and action. A text is also validated by its context within a community of faith. This brings us to our last guide for reading.

3. CELEBRATE AND LIVE THE TEXT WITHIN A COMMUNITY OF FAITH

Reading a biblical text within a community provides a context for the sharing and comparing of interpretations. This is a support, as well as a corrective for our individual efforts to read the Bible. A text often comes alive for us as we listen to another's insights into it. At other times, a community will challenge and clarify an

interpretation we have given to a particular passage. Community is also the context for two intrinsic elements in understanding the word of God: celebration and action. In his 1979 presidential address to the Catholic Biblical Association, "Hermeneutics and the Teaching of Scripture," George T. Montague includes celebration and action as the final steps in interpreting and teaching Scripture. On the importance of celebration for understanding, he says:

> Most of the biblical texts, as most religious texts in general, were created in one way or another as scripts for celebration, and thus there is a surplus of meaning which the text, like the tip of the iceberg, only suggests, and which reliving in ritual alone can reveal. (Montague 16)

For many Christians of earlier ages it was preaching and ritual, cathedral windows and morality plays, not the study of the text, which completed their circle of understanding. The biblical passages are meant to be read, prayed, sung, dramatized. This is done best in a community of believers.

The final test of the Christian community's understanding of a biblical text is the living of its truth. As James and John insist in their New Testament letters, we must learn to do the truth in love. Action within a community of faith alone enable us to understand the final meaning of a passage. Sandra Schneiders concludes her interpretation of the foot washing scene in John 13:1-20 by stressing that one aspect of a valid interpretation of the scene is its significance for contemporary disciple of Jesus. Jesus' washing of the disciples' feet enables us to understand Christian ministry "as a participation in Jesus' work of transforming the sinful structures of domination operative in human society according to the model of friendship expressing itself in joyful mutual service unto death." (Schneiders 91) We have not completely understood Scripture until it transforms us. We have not asked the right questions of the Scriptures until they question us.

When we read the Bible within a community of faith we also discover that these texts continually undergo reinterpretation. A study of the history of texts shows us how they have spoken to and been shaped by new situations. Phyllis Trible in her study, *God and the Rhetoric of Sexuality*, follows what she calls "the pilgrimage of an ancient portrait of God," the text of Exodus 34:6-7:

> Yahweh, Yahweh, a God merciful and gracious, slow to anger, and abounding in loyalty and faithfulness, keeping loyalty for thousands, forgiving iniquity and transgression and sin, but who will by no means clear the guilty, visiting the iniquity of the ancestors upon the children and the children's children, to the third and fourth generation. (RSV translation)

The text holds in tension the punishment and the love of God. Trible shows how different formulations of it appeared in different settings of Israel's history. Moses is depicted as repeating the portrait of God in a prayer, omitting a few phrases (Num 14:8). Jeremiah quotes a condensed version of it as a prayer (Jer 32:18). With the prophet Joel, all the references to the anger of God disappear from the passage (Jl 2:13). The psalmists repeat and paraphrase the passage, fitting it in each case to a particular occasion and experience, whether it be thanksgiving, hymn, or individual lament (Ps 111:4; 112:4; 145:8). After the exile the passage becomes a message of comfort to a defeated people, having lost its allusions to the punishing God (Na 1:5).

Following the journey of this text within Israel's story shows us that interpretation invites us to participate in the movement of a biblical text. The word of God lives by dynamic analogy. A text has been interpreted in the community of faith over many generations, and one generation my discover something that another has missed. The text speaks to different hearers in different contexts and reveals a variety of methodologies: confession, additions, omission, irony. The pilgrimage of such a text is a clue to the pilgrimage of the Bible in the world. The history of biblical passages shows us how the text comes to life for a community of faith, and gives us clues to the dynamic nature of the word of God which bridges historical gaps.

This is what is meant by *hearing* the Word. John's Gospel speaks of such hearing as dwelling or remaining in God's word.

> To the Jews who believed in him Jesus said: 'If you make my word your home you will indeed be my disciples, you will learn the truth and the truth will make you free' (8:31-32).

When we dwell in the Word, making it our home, it becomes a living power in our lives. Since God's self-disclosure takes place in symbol, dwelling in the Word is an act of the imagination. We do not try to put ourselves back into past history. We rely on what William Beardslee refers to as a story's capacity to bring "a remembered past into the present" (Beardslee 16). John also stresses that abiding in God's word is intimately connected with keeping the commandments in a spirit of love (15:10). We begin with attentive listening to the Word itself, in the context of a community of ritual and action. We use all the guidance that literary and historical criticism can provide for hearing the Word. Then the final test of our understanding of Scripture is our willingness to witness to it in life.

END NOTES

[1] My discussion is based on the approach to this passage by Walter Vogels, "Structural Analysis and Pastoral Work," *Lumen Vitae* 33/4 (1978): 482-492.

[2] For helpful suggestions on such reading see Robert Alter, *The Art of Biblical Narrative* (New York: Basic, 1981), and Gerhard Lohfink, *The Bible: Now I Get It!* (New York: Doubleday, 1979): 84-92.

WORKS CITED

Beardslee, William. *Literary Criticism of the New Testament*. Philadelphia: Fortress, 1970.

Gadamer, Hans-George. *Truth and Method*. New York: Seabury, 1975.

Landy, Francis. "The Song of Songs and the Garden of Eden." *Journal of Biblical Literature* 98/4 (December 1979).

Montague, George T. "Hermeneutics and the Teaching of Scripture." *Catholic Biblical Quarterly* 41/1 (January 1979).

Rauber, D.F. "Literary Values in the Book of Ruth." *Journal of Biblical Literature* 89 (March 1970).

Ricoeur, Paul. *Interpretation Theory: Discourse and the Surplus of Meaning.* Fort Worth: Texas Christian UP, 1976.

Schneiders, Sandra. "The Foot Washing (John 13:1-20): An Experiment in Hermeneutics." *Catholic Biblical Quarterly* 43/1 (January 1981).

Trible, Phyllis. *God and the Rhetoric of Sexuality.* Philadelphia: Fortress, 1978.

Weisel, Elie. *Souls on Fire.* New York: Vintage, 1973

————. *Messengers of God: Biblical Portraits & Legends.* Translated by Marion Wiesel. New York: Random, 1976.

Chapter 8

Aids for Preparing Liturgical Celebrations

B. Liturgical Drama

By Michael E. Moynahan, SJ

I. WHAT IS IT?

If I were to draw a picture depicting a typical Roman Catholic liturgy, it would consist of a gigantic mouth overwhelming a tiny ear. Talk! Talk! Talk! So much of our liturgy is simply verbal, and poor verbiage at that! As celebrators of God's covenant we have lost contact with our visual and ritual roots. Liturgical drama is an attempt to rediscover them.

Liturgical drama tries to engage the whole person, not just our ears. It attempts to allow us to respond totally to the Good News. This means not just in a logical or reasonable way, but as a thinking/feeling person. Liturgical drama tries, with all the means available, to let the Word become flesh in the nineties. Through the use of drama, in the context of the liturgy, we attempt to communicate the Word of God as clearly and as powerfully as possible.

Jesus used stories (parables) in his day to spark the imaginations of his audience and capture their hearts. His images were clear, familiar, and effective. He used the best means available to communicate his message. Jesus touched people. He comforted them. He spoke to them. He listened to them. He laughed, got angry, and enjoyed a party as much as the next fellow.

Dramatization is one of the means we have been given whereby we can capture some of the warmth, the feeling and the spirit of the man Jesus. Just as Jesus' stories could captivate his audiences and communicate his message, so too dramatizations are powerful modern means for us to reclaim congregations and allow the Good News to be proclaimed in new and powerful ways.

ACTIONS SPEAK LOUDER THAN WORDS

At the last supper, before Jesus began his teaching on love and service, St. John tells us that he got up from the table and washed the feet of his friends. After this ritual of service, and only after it, did Jesus talk to his friends about the significance of his actions. After washing he talked about why he washed.

Actions so often say more than mere words. And they do not always have to substitute. It does not have to be an "either/or" situation with words and dramatic action. They can support one another and in this way allow the Word to be proclaimed more effectively.

We can talk about love and we can actually love. It is the difference between homilizing and dramatizing. "Talk is cheap. Whisky costs money!" "Put your money where your mouth is!" "Put up or shut up!" These slogans point to the possible disparity between what we say and what we do. Jesus' death on the cross was the most eloquent and moving statement he could make about love for someone else. It paled in one sense, and yet reinforced and substantiated everything he had ever said about love.

Week after week we hear another installment from one of the four Gospel writers. Out of habit we nod our heads as Jesus continues to do his good deeds. Overworked medium and poor transmission combine each week to uncover new ways of rendering the Good News impotent. Jesus not only spoke about caring for others, he showed us how to care by giving sight to the blind, by restoring hearing to the deaf, speech to the dumb, strength of legs to the lame and feeling to the stone-hearted. How much of this is conveyed or affects us through the Sunday rendering of the Gospel?

ENGAGEMENT

There is a California Jesuit who travels around the country with his little circus. His name is Father Nick Weber. His work is creator, director, and ringmaster for the smallest circus in the world: the Royal Lichtenstein Quarter Ring Side Walk Circus. I had the opportunity of working three months with him. During that time I experiences how you can touch people, heal people through drama and the circus.

In the circus we engaged not just the congregation's ears, but their eyes, their smell, their feelings, in a word - the heart. And in this way we somehow freed their spirit to respond and celebrate. We taught them by showing them how wonderful surprise is: Christmas trees from crumpled newspaper, doves from popped balloons, and ducks from oven roasted birds.

The spoken word in the circus was appropriately wedded to action. The result was learning, laughing, shedding a tear of melancholy or joy, celebrating life, and somehow leaving the circus feeling richer and wiser than when you came. Can the same be said by those who attend our Sunday liturgies? Are they really celebrations? How many of our worshippers do we engage in liturgy? Just the head or the whole person?

We have to engage more than the ears and minds of our worshippers. The more senses engaged in liturgy, the more powerful and complete the liturgical experience can be. And this is no magic formula. It is just good sense.

Drama uses many senses and appeals to the complete person. Consider the ways Jesus healed people - word and action, speaking and touching. Words can be misleading, even equivocal at times. Actions, gestures, a worked-out mime, are all powerful proclamations in their clarity, brevity, and simplicity.

II. TYPES OF LITURGICAL DRAMA

There are at least seven types of liturgical drama. Some forms run dangerously close, if not over, into another's area. There can be multiple variations in specific kinds of liturgical drama. We will examine some of the possibilities as we look at each drama type. The seven forms of drama are: interpretive proclamation, group interpretive proclamation, mime, improvisation, psycho-drama, scene or story dramatizations, and the total dramatic liturgical experience. Let's take a look now at each form and its potential liturgical use.

1. *Interpretive proclamation* consists of one person vocally presenting, interpreting, and proclaiming the scriptural Good News to us. It is more than a dull recitation of meaningless words and phrases. It is not mumbling or bungling your way through an unfamiliar passage from the Bible. It is using all the gifts God has given you in the range, depth, pitch, and resonance of your voice and helping the Word come to life.

Too often, timid lectors feel any type of reading that departs from deadening monotone is totally out of place. Many potential good lectors are unfairly intimidated by those who might fault his or her energetic proclamation as "over-doing it," "hamming it up," "acting," "entertaining us instead of helping us to pray." We have to remember that when our congregation has been hypnotized, lulled into an etherizing sleep by the monotonous murmurings of the unskilled at the lectern, they will be shocked and disturbed by any Scripture that falls upon their ears above a whisper. Perhaps if we had some men and women lectors who would use their voices fully to proclaim God's Word to us, we would put down those distracting and menacing missalettes once and for all.

Interpretive proclamation is evocative. It demands a response. Through it, a skilled lector can vocally command the attention of the congregation and dispose them to listening and responding to the Word of God. He or she can try to capture the different characters with his or her voice, for example, the calmness and straightforwardness of the narrator, the desperation of the Canaanite woman, the gentleness or surprise of Jesus. Where there is only one character, as found in the discourses of St. John's Gospel or in the book of the prophet Isaiah, the lector should try to capture the mood with his voice. He or she might also try to tip us off, through what he or she emphasizes, to the focus of the homily.

2. *Group interpretive proclamations* involve a number of people taking the different parts of a piece of Scripture, generally from the Gospels. This is something like the reader's theater. It helps the gospel scene come to life through the rich resource of a number of gifted voices in the congregation. The vocal interpretation sparks our imagination and depicts for us, in broad strokes, the details of a particular scriptural encounter between God and man.

An example of a group interpretive proclamation is the Gospel for the twentieth Sunday of the year. It could involve participation of five to seven voices. The passage deals with Jesus healing the daughter of the Canaanite women. The character voices would be the narrator, Jesus, the Canaanite woman, and at least two disciples.

What advantage does a group interpretive proclamation have over a simple reading? First of all, different voices establish much more easily the presence of different characters. Secondly, the total group effort helps create and lead the congregation in a veritable contemplation of the gospel scene. Although it will take some getting use to, congregations will be much more responsive to these types of proclamations.

Do not be afraid to print up and include parts for the entire congregation. This is certainly encouraged and done at times like Good Friday's proclamation of the Lord's passion. Whenever a Scripture reading calls for a crowd part, a group of scribes or pharisees, townspeople or whatever, involve your congregation. Invite them not just to watch and listen but to participate.

Contemporary plays can also enhance our worship. On special occasions, if a particular scene from a play complements the theme of your celebration, try the group interpretive proclamation technique on it too.

3. A third type of liturgical drama is *mime* or *pantomime*. In this form of drama, a story is generally told without words by means of bodily and facial movements. Marcel Marceau is the most publicized and popular pantomimist in this country. Through mime he creates a complete imaginary world or scene right before our eyes. He proclaims his story through the eloquent communication of his bodily movements and gestures.

There are a number of ways in which mime can be used in liturgy today. To begin with, there is the completely silent mime. Generally, after a reading, a character comes out with a placard which introduces the mime. If your reading was the parable of the prodigal son, your placard might simply read "Father and Sons."

After the mime has been introduced, the players, if you already in position, come in and begin the action of the mime. They use no words, but their meaning, their communication is loud and clear. The mimers can make visible the gospel scene and compound its impact on us.

There is a strange but powerful dynamism in liturgical mime. We are drawn into the scene by the characters. They imaginatively create the whole incident and pull us into the gospel scene not as spectators but participators. Nuances of meaning and feeling are conveyed by the pantomimist in ways simple words could never hope to communicate.

Another way to use mime is with some background music. In this way the music can help you create the mood of mime. Music is yet another powerful dramatic tool of communication. There is a wealth of music, classical and modern, to help you capture and create and translate for your congregation feelings of crisis, sadness, melancholy, and joy.

Still another form of mime would employ a narrative text. If your theme was "giving" you might enact Shel Silverstein's *The Giving Tree*. One person could narrate the story while two others would mime the parts of the tree and the little boy. This can be used very effectively at both children's and adult liturgies. You could use this type of narrative mime with any number of fairy tales that touch on different themes for celebration.

Liturgical mimes are of three types. They can be based on Scripture, on extra-biblical readings (for example, fairy tales), or they can be "spin-off" mimes. In the first two, the action is somewhat limited and clearly defined by the mime's respective narration (script). The third type does need a word of explanation.

A "spin-off" mime consists of taking the theme, the message or point of a particular piece of Scripture, and contemporizing its meaning for a given congregation. Here is an example of what I am talking about. The scripture scene is Jesus calming the storm at sea. This particular piece of Scripture deals with the fear of the disciples, the hostile external environment, Jesus' surprise at his friends' little faith, Jesus' care for them by calming the storm and quieting their fears, and finally the disciples' amazement. We would take any one of these elements and weave a contemporary mime.

How would you go about it? The place to begin is by a group of planners brainstorming. After reading the piece of Scripture toss around some questions and ideas. From these the mime will grow. What would be some contemporary storms we find ourselves in? How do we feel abandoned? What are the ways Jesus quiets our fears? How do we know he is present? How does he challenge our faith? It is, at once, a challenge to translate imaginatively the Gospel into everyday life situations, as well as an opportunity to proclaim contemporarily that the Word of God is still Good News.

4. *Improvisation* is the next type of liturgical drama. To improvise is to create or invent on the spot. It is taking what is at hand and weaving from it a scenario or story. To use improvisation effectively at liturgy takes much time, work, and discipline. The improvisation is actually set when it is done in the context of the liturgy. A group of planners or players has had the freedom to create and play with an idea or theme long before the liturgy takes place. They have worked with it, refined it, and concretized it. In effect, it has been scripted (set down) by the time it is enacted.

What would be an example of a liturgical improvisation? If the gospel passage dealt with the call of one or a number of disciples, you might deal with the theme of "calls" in our lives and how we "answer" them. How we respond to everyday calls, demands placed on our time, attention and energy, will give us an idea of how well we can and do respond to the ways the Lord calls us in our lives.

I have found the use of this form of liturgical drama, oftentimes as a homily, to be a powerful and moving experience for a congregation. It certainly should be used on occasion as a possible liturgical alternative option. But give yourself plenty of time. Make sure you start long before a liturgy is scheduled so you have time to create, refine, and concretize your improvisations.

5. An adapted form is *psycho-drama*, when used at liturgy, can prove effective. Psycho-drama is an improvised dramatization. It is used quite a bit in family or group counseling where tensions and disagreements develop between members. It is designed to allow resolution of conflicts and heightened awareness of the social complexity of issues for one or more of the participants. The plot is abstracted from the player's life history.

Now liturgy is not a counseling session. So the way to use psycho-drama in the context of the liturgy is much along the lines of an improvisation. Players take the roles of what would be real-life psycho-drama participants. The developed plot focuses on areas of conflict for average families, Christians, or worshipping groups.

A group of people used this form of drama effectively in a series on the Ten Commandments. The Sunday that "Honor thy father and mother" was treated, we used some psycho-drama. There were two players: a father and a son. The father had recently discovered drugs in his son's room. When the son came home, the father wanted to talk. Actually he wanted to punish the living daylights out of him. When the father confronted his son, the son responded with anger and dismay that the dad would have searched his room. The two, through yells and screams, proceeded to communicate ineffectively with one another.

What the congregation witnessed was a ritual of two wounded animals. Both father and son felt betrayed. What they wanted to do was communicate. What neither could see was that their strong feelings of anger and betrayal prevented them from really listening to one another. They could only strike one another verbally in the way they felt stricken.

The players never knew when the little drama would end. They had to act it out, if need be, to its conclusion. But shortly after the major issues and feelings surfaced, the celebrant rang a bell. Father and son returned to their respective places. For the homily, the celebrant stood between the father and the son and explained the nature of reverence: reverence of a son for his father, and of a father for his son. He developed the suffering and cost of genuine respect and trust. The very human problems that stand in the way of son-loving father and father-trusting son. He made the congregation aware of the complexity and difficulty of the fourth commandment.

Father and son flanked the celebrant for the rest of the liturgy. The conflict was still partially unresolved. At the kiss of peace, the celebrant, after a brief exhortation to both father and son about Christian forgiveness, facilitated the reconciliation of the two. Celebrant, father, and son then shared this peace with the entire congregation.

6. A sixth type of liturgical drama is what I call the *scenario* or *story dramatization*. This involves the acting out of a short scenario by different characters. This form differs from the group interpretive proclamation. In the group proclamation you simply spark the imagination of your congregation vocally. In the story dramatization all the actor's tools are employed: body and voice.

One type of story drama might be a scene from a play. A full scene might be too long. So it might be a scenic excerpt. If you can find a good translation, or if your congregation would not be put off by Old English, there are countless medieval miracle and morality plays. They could be especially effective during the Christmas, Lent, and Easter seasons and other appropriate occasions.

Another possibility would be to resituate a piece of Scripture by creating a story dramatization. Take, for instance, the story of the Good Samaritan. Bring it up to date. Who would be a modern parallel to the Samaritan? To the doctor of the law? To the priest? What would be the equivalent of the Road to Jericho? The incident of the New York woman who was stabbed to death in her own front yard while frightened neighbors looked on is a frighteningly similar situation. Human nature is still human nature. Christ still calls us to be involved and we pass him by, wounded on the road, for the very best of reasons.

Try dramatizing a fairy tale or story. There is plenty of literature available. One of Aesop's fables could be done briefly but powerfully. There are many good Sufi stories that lend themselves to dramatization. Idries Shah has edited a number of volumes of them. And Martin Buber has shared a number of excellent Hasidic teaching stories. All are fine material for dramatization.

Perhaps the most challenging type of story dramatization is the one you create and write yourselves. It should be based on some theme you are celebrating.

7. The final type of liturgical drama is what I like to refer to as the *total dramatic liturgical experience*. Simply put, it is all the possibilities during the celebration of Holy Week that offer themselves for dramatization. Palm Sunday, Holy Thursday, Good Friday, and Easter Vigil are all dramatically rich. Each year it is a new challenge to allow some of Holy Week's dramatic richness and evocative power to emerge.

You can create a great deal of dramatization on Good Friday. One example is during the proclamation of the Passion. Year after year we hear the same Gospel proclaimed. You can mime the Passion. You can design and execute a mime called "Come Passion" and try to capture not only the terrible physical suffering and remarkable love found in the Passion, but the personal invitation Jesus makes to each of us to enter into his suffering and dying so we can share the real joy of resurrection.

The dramatic possibilities of Holy Week are many and varied. All you need to do is gather a group of imaginative and energetic people. Give yourselves plenty of time. Get in touch with the thematic movement of each day. Then create, refine, concretize, and execute.

III. WHERE CAN YOU USE IT?

You can use liturgical drama in different parts of the liturgy. In the present structure of the Mass, the liturgy of the Word best lends itself to dramatization. The readings and homily are primary moments in the liturgy of the Word. Dramatizations could be effectively used here. Every reading should be at least interpretively proclaimed. However, let me add a word of caution. Using more than one dramatization at a liturgy can diminish its effectiveness as well as overload the liturgy.

Respect the rhythm and movements of the liturgy of the Word and the liturgy of the Eucharist. Avoid drawing undue attention to parts of the liturgy that are of only secondary importance. Try to heighten and emphasize through dramatization those parts of the liturgy that are of primary importance. Drama is an excellent tool to strengthen and support your liturgical proclamations.

Liturgy planners should not be afraid to explore all liturgical possibilities. If you have a good grasp of where your congregation is, you will not be in danger of pushing them beyond their limits. Remember that a community of worshippers must be led along slowly but surely. The criteria must always be whether what we do helps the congregation celebrate more fully God's saving action in our lives. Certain themes and occasions in the liturgical year demand a more visible and forceful proclamation of this Good News. Dramatizations directed by the right hands and executed by the right bodies and voices can be a valuable tool to accomplish this.

We have only mentioned a few of our potential options. Besides using liturgical drama in the context of the Penance rite, to help proclaim a reading, or as an alternative to the spoken homily, dramatizations might be used in a number of other places. Processions in and out of church provide excellent opportunities to dramatize.

The eucharistic acclamation offers us yet another opportunity for dramatization. Have you ever tried a non-verbal (dramatized) triple Amen at the conclusion of the eucharistic prayer? At the conclusion of the doxology, as the people are sitting, have them extend their hands palms-up in front of them. This gesture of offering is the gesture of even more emphatic offering. This constitutes the second Amen. Finally, after another significant pause, the whole congregation rises and, with hands still palms-up, extends them fully in front, the concluding, Amen. And what you have is a non-verbal dramatization. The effect is powerfully moving.

Still another possibility might be found at the kiss of peace or during the communion meditation. Stretching the imagination even further, what about a non-verbal eucharistic prayer? Difficult? Yes! Impossible? No! All these different moments in the Mass offer themselves for dramatization. It would be good, though, to start with something simple and workable, especially within the context of the liturgy of the word.

IV. DON'T FORGET

Here are some important guidelines to keep in mind when utilizing drama. Symbols that are not clear are poor symbols at best and probably no symbols at all. Drama that fails to communicate is poor drama, especially in the context of the liturgy. If you have to explain it, you have done something wrong.

In selecting and using dramatic forms, ask yourselves the following questions.

1. *What is it you want to say? Is it clear in your own mind first?*
2. *How do you want to say it or proclaim it? (e.g. mime, improvisation, etc.)*
3. *Is this the best possible way to communicate it? Would a mime be better than an improvisation? Or would a group interpretive proclamation be better than a dramatized story?*
4. *Do you communicate what you want to communicate? Is it clear?*
5. *Do you say it as economically as possible? Do you say no more nor less than you want to say? Is it brief?*
6. *Is your communication uncluttered and unencumbered? Is it simple?*
7. *And, as always, the final question and gauge: What do people hear you saying? What do they see you doing? What is actually communicated?*

Planning and using drama in our liturgies involves hard work. The results, though, are gratifying. Liturgical drama can help congregations participate and pray wholly. It is high time we realize that God's Word is addressed to the whole person, not just the brain and ear. The more fully we communicate the Good News, the more powerful this proclamation will be. Rediscovering the dramatic possibilities in our liturgy is simply using all God has given us — body, voice, heart, mind, and spirit — to help the Word become flesh again in our lives.

Chapter 8

Aids for Preparing Liturgical Celebrations

C. Symbols and Rituals

By Janet Schaffran and Pat Kozak

Ritual is an integral part of life, common to all creatures. It provides the actions and forms through which people meet, carry out social activities, celebrate, and commemorate. Whether actions performed appear casual or dramatic, sacred or secular, they express a meaning and significance that extend beyond the particular event itself.

Rituals express the truths by which we live, the relationships and beliefs that underlie our lives. Rituals, like the way we greet each other, the blessing before sharing a meal, the expression of thanks when receiving a gift, the spoken or kissed "good night" at the end of the day, all carry a significance greater than mere social conformity.

As a faith community, we have a need for rituals that convey the power and significance of the present moment and situate that moment within the context of our shared faith. One such example is the long held ritual we celebrate on the occasion of a birthday. I still recall the third birthday of a nephew. The family, parents, siblings, aunts, and uncles were gathered around the table while the three-year-old celebrant stood perched on a chair, face aglow with the candlelight. He looked excitedly from face to face while we sang to him. When he was finally told, "Make a wish!" the child, with sheer delight, blew out the candles to the sound of enthusiastic applause. The mystery of life was once more celebrated. Given gratuitously, age is not merited or earned in any way. Life and time are gifts of a gracious God, witnessed to and celebrated by those who are bonded in love.

It may be necessary to adapt the action or the ritual to allow for further and more meaningful participation. It may be helpful to change the setting, the physical arrangements, in order to accommodate the number of people and to enable their meaningful and comfortable presence. It might be advantageous to prepare the place of the gathering to make the atmosphere more conducive and supportive of the ritual prayer.

We are sensual people and the more our senses are involved, the more likely we are to be fully involved as whole persons. So color, lighting, acoustics, movement, seating, and logistics all merit some attention. Their particular use and adaptation will be influenced by the words and style of the prayer, by the occasion of the gathering, by the number of people present, and by the practical limitations of space, time, and resources. Part II will offer specific examples and suggest ways in which these concerns might be expressed.

One last comment regarding the variety of elements involved in any ritual. There is a need today to reaffirm the human, to celebrate the natural wisdom and beauty to be found within creation. It is a way of giving witness to our faith that "because of creation, and still more the Incarnation, nothing is profane." The human person is made in the image of God and continues to reveal divinity in and through the sometimes subtle, always profound mystery of humanity. The created universe, since its first birthing, was charged with the breath and Spirit of God. "It was good" from its very origin. The "stuff" of our physical lives, our bodies and our world, is sacred. The more we can incorporate and express this belief in our common prayer, the greater the capacity this prayer possesses to root us in the goodness and mystery of our God.

The use of gesture and movement, of dance and mime, restores a connectedness with our own bodies. The use of earth symbols such as water and air, earth and fire, re-establishes our rootedness in this awesome and fragile planet on which we make our home.

We are in need of a greater ability, perhaps even a greater willingness, to live symbolically. However, this calls for some caution because living symbolically does not mean that we surround ourselves with objects and signs or claim that the ultimate revelation has been given in each and every event of our lives. An appreciation of symbols requires a reflective presence, a realization that there is always more present than what meets the eye. It requires that we recognize that God has become involved with us and in our world, and that our human experience, in the context of such faith, has lasting significance.

If rituals are to be meaningful, persons must first believe that their experiences are true and worthy of reflection. These reflected-upon experiences are then shared with the community as stories of faith, and finally, celebrated as experiences of faith, grace, and power. Such celebrations become festivals of incarnation, redemption, and our ongoing resurrection; they mark our own passage to greater and fuller life.

It is important that rituals and symbols not be contrived. If a lot of words are needed to explain a symbol, do not use it. Either the symbol lacks the power and clarity to speak for itself or the experience of the community is limited and they are unable to make the connection that links ritual with life.

Go slowly at first. Use what is most common and natural, what is already experientially part of people's life: water, light, fire, darkness, earth, bread, and wine. Build on these to enable people to slow down the inner pace of their lives and to recognize a rhythm and truth there. This enables an appreciation of the symbolic as well as the ability to express oneself and one's faith in ritual. This eventual expression of faith is a strengthening of the individual and of the community.

We are long overdue for a change, for movement from the too-often-sterile places and styles of prayer, devoid of any sign of a good and gracious God. We are long overdue for a change, for movement from the too-often-inhospitable places and styles of prayer, where "community" and "family" are far from the experience of the believers who gather. We are long overdue for a change, for movement from the too frequent uniformity of our worship to a profound sensitivity that acknowledges the exquisite beauty and mystery of our humanness, the richness of our diversity, and our capacity to manifest the power and glory of God.

There is good reason to believe that this long overdue change can begin now; in fact, it has already begun. Listed below are common themes in prayer. For each theme possible symbols and rituals are indicated.

Birth and Naming
Symbols: Egg, balloons, earth (soil or clay), personally naming another, a mirror to image self, a tree, pictures of contemporary prophetic people.

Ritual: Telling what your name means or the ritual expression of a clown.

Hope
Symbols: Clover (three- or four-leaf), sheafs of wheat, wildflowers, globe (hope for global awareness), seeds, evergreen branches, shells, a wreath entwined with weeds and flowers, a bird, Japanese cranes.

Rituals: Mime, body movement expressing reaching out, circular movements.

Justice-Seeking People
Symbols: A globe or large map, clippings of recent newspaper articles, a bag of clothes.

Rituals: Four readers for the service— one from the North, South, East, and West — sharing a variety of breads and crackers representing diversity of peoples and cultures.

Death - Life
Symbols: Fall leaves, pictures of death/life, wall-hanging or tapestry from various countries (for example, El Salvador, Brazil, Norther Ireland), a wreath, a stain of blood, water, branches, a red piece of cloth, wind and light, pictures or symbols "in memory of" experiences of people.

Rituals: Use of fire to consume or transform, moving from one prayer space to another - symbolizing "new life."

New Life
Symbols: Brightly colored eggs, flowing water, flowers, colored sashes from various cultures, food, Bible.

Rituals: Lighting fire, circle dance rituals, gesture prayer outside facing the sun, ritual sharing of what give life, what is life-giving today for you.

Service
Symbols: Wine, bread, foods that are festive, hospitality, God's Word, maypole, garden tools, wood carving tools, crafts, painted faces, cord or twine symbolizing weaving together lives of service, ceramic pots, homemade shawl.

Rituals: Praying a blessing over each other, washing of hands, cooking a simple meal and inviting another and eating together.

Chapter 8

Aids for Preparing Liturgical Celebrations

D. Inclusive Language

By Janet Schaffran and Pat Kozak

Words are one of the primary ways by which we connect with each other. We come to communicate via words; we come to understanding, even to solidarity, through the not-so-simple ways in which sounds are arranged in sequence. Much of this is arbitrary. How did one word come to mean one thing and not another? Why is one word appropriate and another not? To what degree are words and their meanings a matter of social convention?

Inclusive language is not a fad. It is not this year's "cause," to be soon replaced by another. The growing use of inclusive language is the result of a serious commitment on the part of many people to use words more responsibly, to speak more precisely, and to communicate more truthfully and sensitively.

Many books have been written concerning the development of language from a variety of perspectives. For the interested reader, they are well worth the time and effort to read and integrate. It is our intention, however, simply to address the questions, "Why do we bother with inclusive language?" and "How much is involved in this 'inclusivity'?"

We are affected both consciously and unconsciously by the language we hear and use. It would seem that repeated use of words develops a certain immunity, a resistance to their meaning and impact. Such words, then, have minimal effect: crass words no longer jar us, slang becomes acceptable, scientific and military terms are adapted to daily experiences without notice. However, there is much to suggest that this is not the case. We are not unaffected by words, and our seeming freedom and ease with particular usage is perhaps more the result of numbness and verbal satiation than matured sensitivity.

Language is always influential and formative, but it may be especially influential in times of prayer, because at these times, ideally, the whole person is involved - through speech and hearing, through sight and touch and movement.

People are often more relaxed, receptive, less on guard and hence more susceptible to the variety of messages being conveyed. More of the experience is likely to be absorbed, both consciously and unconsciously. This receptivity may facilitate an experience of community support, a recognition of the holiness of God, or a realization of the beauty of our own humanness. However, such positive experiences are not always the result.

Imagine a concelebrated liturgy in a church where the vast majority of worshippers are black. Imagine this liturgy concelebrated by five white male priests, gathered around the altar, wearing colorful vestments and proclaiming, "We are a holy race, a royal priesthood..." (Preface to the Fourth Eucharistic Prayer, *Roman Liturgy*). What does a black child see and experience at such a liturgy? White men proclaiming that they are a holy race? Are blacks unholy? Unworthy? What does a young black girl see and experience? She sees only men, only white men, dressed in special robes. Can only white men belong to this holy race, to this royalty and priesthood? Are all blacks and all women unholy and unworthy?

In this experience, the reason for the concelebration does not matter. The origin of the particular translation of the Eucharistic prayer or its tradition does not matter. The richness of the original Scripture from which the passage was drawn does not matter. These reasons and insights are all unknown to the child. In this situation, the question remains: What does the black child or adult experience at this liturgy? The question is significant because liturgy is not intended to be first and foremost a cognitive experience. It is, instead, an experience and expression of faith.

What do we expect a child to understand when we teach that "God loved men so much that He himself was born a man in order to come to earth and be with us"? Are we unconsciously teaching that it is better to be a man than a woman? If God, who is wise, chose to become a man, did God choose the better of two options?

We are increasingly aware of the impact that verbal abuse, insulting name-calling, and minimizing humor can have on a person in the development of self-concept or in the perception of that person's environment. Non-inclusive language does similar damage. An unwillingness on the part of Church people to use inclusive language is especially difficult to understand because of all the times and places to use words responsibly and sensitively, common prayer and public worship would seem to merit a priority of care and attention.

What about the charge that inclusive language is simply an overreaction? Doesn't everyone already understand what is meant by the words used so that any change in language is really unnecessary?

What about "We hold these truths to be self-evident, that all men are created equal...with certain inalienable rights?" If our "fore-fathers" who wrote these words understood "men" to be inclusive of women, why did it require a constitutional amendment for women to vote? If "men" is understood to mean all people, why did it take years of struggle, congressional legislation, and police protection for black sisters and brothers to be able to vote? The truth is that "men" has not always been an inclusive term and continues even today to be restrictive in meaning. In the interests of clarity and charity, the use of inclusive language is necessary.

What about the charge of "tradition?" After all, we have always said it this way. People have grown accustomed to it and have some feeling about it.

This charge holds a strange mixture of fact and fiction, of merit and nonsense. Simple convention does not constitute a tradition, and having done something before should never be the primary reason for doing it again. The question needs to be asked: What truth or value does this action or passage express? It would seem more respectful of persons to assume their desire to communicate honestly and clearly rather than assume their inability or unwillingness to change and grow.

What about the charge "but the author wrote it this way and a change in the text will destroy the poetry and flow of the passage?"

It is important to safeguard the quality of a translation and to preserve the delicacy of style of a particular text. And it is possible to do this. It is possible to modify the wording in a way that maintains the harmony and grace of a passage and at the same time avoids jarring the reader or listener with an uneven or unnatural paraphrase. Any author must necessarily write from within a particular culture. His or her writing may well represent the best of that culture. Adapting the language of a given passage may very possibly be more consistent with the author's efforts to communicate sensitively than an insistence on retaining exclusive and inaccurate expressions. It is hard to imagine that the great writers, preachers, composers, and believers of earlier times, among them, Jesus, Sojourner Truth, Anne Hutchinson, and John XXIII would object.

What about the charge that changing the language is inconvenient?

It is true. It is time-consuming and it is inconvenient. And so too is living the Gospel. Something is sadly missing when inconvenience becomes the criterion for our actions.

Any word, any language, is a human invention. It has not come down directly from "on high," but rather out of the "stuff" of our human situation, human history, and human cultures. Our hearts, our lives, our words, and our world are all on the way, all in process of redemption and transformation. The only constant word is the Word made flesh, and that is the one Word that crosses cultures and time. That Word, that person, still calls us to conversion and to change.

In the following section, as well as in the prayer services themselves, we offer examples of common changes toward inclusive language for use in prayer.

As anyone who has struggled to change non-inclusive language knows, it is often more difficult to adapt language than it first appears. The choice of revision will first depend upon the context. For example, the number of syllables and the accent are important to note if the change is to be made is in a song. A casual gathering of believers will allow some revisions that would be inappropriate in a formal assembly, while the literary style of the passage, particularly poetry, will dictate some words rather than others.

Changes in language can be divided into four types:

1. Adding a female reference to an exclusively male reference, for example, adding "and sisters" to "brothers," or changing "he" or "his" to "he/she" and "his/her."
2. Deleting of the exclusive word, for example, changing "we have know his mercy" to "we have known mercy."
3. Substituting an appropriate synonym, for example, "mankind" becomes

"humankind," "kinsmen" becomes "kinspeople," "family," or "relatives."
4. Finding an alternate way of expressing the same concept, for example,
   "Merciful Father" can be changed to "Compassionate God," "God of mercy,"
   "Source of all mercy"; or the line "And crown thy good with brotherhood"
   might be changed to "And make of us one family."

The following are examples of changes that can be made to incorporate inclusive language into common prayer. While not all-encompassing, they offer suggestions for options in language change.

If the text reads: God...he made the heavens
Change to: God...you made the heavens; God...who made the heavens

If the text reads: God...his love is everlasting
Change to: God...whose love is everlasting; God...your love is everlasting;
God...this love is everlasting

If the text reads: We have known his mercy
Change to: We have known God's mercy; We have known your mercy; We have known this mercy; We have known mercy

If the text reads: From the power of sinful men
Change to: Power of sinful men and women; power of sin; power of the sinful; power of sinful ones

If the text reads: This man ... his
Change to: Man and woman...their; they...their; people...their; all...their

If the text reads: Spokesman
Change to: Spokesperson; representative

If the text reads: Clergyman
Change to: Clergyperson; minister; cleric

If the text reads: God become man
Change to: God became human; The one who was divine became human

If the text reads: Brotherhood
Change to: Family; unity

If the text reads: Son
Change to: Son and daughter; child/children; first-born (if appropriate)

If the text reads: Watchman
Change to: Guard; sentry; sentinel

If the text reads: Kingdom of God
Change to: Reign of God; God's dream for all creation

A further guide on the topic of inclusive language is *Cleaning Up Sexist Language*, a booklet published by the Eighth Day Center in Chicago. It offers a thorough rationale for and extensive practical examples of inclusive language.

Chapter 8

Aids for Preparing
Liturgical Celebrations

E. Cultural Pluralism

By Janet Schaffran and Pat Kozak

What does it mean for us as people of the United States to pray as members of the Church? What does it mean to pray as members of the world community? As a global family? We often use these terms glibly, though sincerely, assuming our own awareness of the beauty and diversity of these communities. We assume a cognitive and affective acceptance of the peoples of these communities.

But is this assumption true? Are we aware of the culturally distinct peoples within our local communities? Are we attentive to the significant numbers of Hispanic, African, Asian, and Native American persons who make their home in the United States? Are we aware that the U.S. population represents only 6 percent of the population of the earth?

And what does this reality have to do with how we pray?

Our prayer is expressive of who we are and what we believe, what we have experienced, and what we hope for. It is important that this "who we are" be understood as broadly as possible. We are a global family and as such share in the wisdom and experience of the entire community of believers. Without this realization, we pray as less than ourselves, lacking an awareness of the power and rootedness and solidarity that could be ours.

What does it mean to pray with an awareness and appreciation of the cultural pluralism that exists within this body of believers? To begin with, it might mean that we pray differently when we pray as a community. When we gather for common prayer or formal worship, we often rely on materials that are highly verbal and minimize feeling and color or the possibility of spontaneous expression. We generally draw on the writings of white persons and make use of white music and white voices, whether spoken or sung. Our prayer services typically manifest a Western system of logic characterized by linear progression and rational tone.

All this is strikingly inconsistent with any avowed appreciation for cultural diversity and pluralism. The occasional inclusion of writings of a South American theologian or Native American poetry or black music, however well intentioned, is sadly inadequate. Sporadic use of these sources only serves to perpetuate a situation of inequality and unconscious prejudice.

If we are to be taken seriously as members of a global family and universal Body of Christ, it is essential that our prayer reflect this identity, at least in our efforts to be multicultural.

How much is necessary? To what limits of pluralism and inclusion are we called? In Psalm 137, we pray, "Though there our captors asked of us lyrics of our songs, and our despoilers urged us to be joyous: `Sing for us the songs of Zion!' How could we sing a song to our God in a foreign land?" This is true of us today as it was for the Israelite more than two thousand years ago. In order to share our prayer we need to feel at home, comfortable, at least minimally at ease with the people and situations around us.

It is important to expand the range of our familiarity beyond the mainstream of our own culture to its margins and marginated people. We need to become familiar with other cultures even within our U.S. American culture.

For example, we might use excerpts from the writings of Martin Luther King, Jr., at times other than Black Culture Week. It is too easy to relegate the wisdom and power of this Christian to one setting or one issue. Why not draw on his writings on faith or perseverance or non-violence or public witness? These values are not restricted to the black community alone; they are his gift to a world community.

What about using the music of Central America and providing the translation and pronunciation? The songs of these present-day ministers of the Word proclaim a belief in the resurrection, a vibrant hope in the face of persecution, and a profound regard for the poor.

Why not use the art and poetry of Africans, of Native Americans, and of Appalachians?

Why not make ample use of the silence of the Quakers and Asian peoples?

Why not make use of the feminine style and image, voice and leadership?

Our liturgy in words and in ritual has become impoverished by our own reliance on the so-called majority culture. Our dependence on one culture has diminished us. We have lost touch with the richness and wisdom of our sisters and brothers throughout the earth.

We have come to rely on and expect certain words, symbols, and rituals used in liturgy. Yet if Eucharist is our daily bread, are not tortillas a clearer, truer sign of daily nourishment in Central America than the traditional eucharistic bread? If we are celebrating the gathering of a community for worship, doesn't the dance of many cultures convey the gathering of people far better than a staid procession? What distinguishes tradition that is imposed on a people from tradition that is expressive of a people and its culture? To whom belongs the right and responsibility to answer such questions?

It is no small thing to begin to try to pray as members of a global family. It would be a hope worthy of our calling and identity if one day sisters and brothers of cultures quite distinct from each other would join together in prayer. All would know they are family. Then as in Psalm 137, we could sing a song to our God. It would be no foreign land in which we are gathered. It would be home.

What follows is a list of themes frequently chosen for community prayer. Opposite each theme is a resource drawn from a culture other than the dominant white American. These resources, songs, readings, and rituals can be incorporated into the prayer experience. If this listing is "successful," it will have sparked still greater creativity in the reader, who will find these resources to be only a beginning.

Theme: God's faithful love
Resource: Relate to the faithful love of the mothers of the disappeared of Central and South America; Colleen Fulmer's song "Mothers of the Plaza de Mayo;" relate to concern for missing children in the United States.

Theme: The power of visioning, dreaming to bring about new creation (or God's Reign of Justice, Peace)
Resource: Excerpts from "I Have a Dream" speech of Martin Luther King Jr., August 28, 1963

Theme: The role of discipline to clarify our focus
Resource: Explanation of the ritual of the "sweat lodge" in Native American cultures

Theme: The human family
Resource: Inviting those present to pray the Lord's Prayer together, encouraging people to pray it aloud in whatever language they know

Theme: Solidarity with the oppressed
Resource: The song "Singing for Our Lives" by Holly Near, adding appropriate verses

Theme: Observance of Hiroshima Day (anniversary of bombing)
Resource: Instrumental music by Japanese composer Kitaro

Theme: Strength of the human spirit against all odds
Resource: Vietnamese poetry set to music in the song "The Rock Will Wear Away," by Cris Williamson

Theme: Stewardship or sanctuary
Resource: Native American readings on the sacredness of the earth, the land as a gift to be shared; use excerpts of "The Land Is Home to Me," a pastoral letter on powerlessness in Appalachia by the Catholic bishops of the region.

Theme: The Gospel as counter-cultural
Resource: Daily headlines

Theme: Perseverance/hope
Resource: Story of Rosa Park's refusal to give up her seat on Montgomery bus and subsequent city-wide bus boycott; its part in the Civil Rights movement.

Theme: God as nurturer, bakerwoman
Resource: breads, foods of many lands and cultures

Theme: Fullness and mystery of life
Resource: Steady drum beat (in many African cultures, the drum expresses the heartbeat of all living things, humans, animals, and the earth mother)

Chapter 9

A Guide to Preparing
Liturgical Celebrations

The following guide is meant to integrate many of the insights and elements of effective liturgy into a series of steps that a liturgy team can use in their work. This guide is designed for preparing eucharistic liturgies, but can be easily adapted to preparing a variety worship experiences (for example, Liturgy of the Hours, adolescent rituals).

Prior to using this guide, please review Chapter 4 - "Improving Worship for Youth," Chapter 6 - "Preparing and Evaluating Worship for Youth," and Chapter 7 - "Qualities and Criteria for Liturgical Celebrations." Chapter 8 - "Aids for Preparing Liturgical Celebrations" is an essential resource of ideas for liturgical celebrations. Be sure to consult the resource guide in Chapter 12 for materials to assist you in preparing liturgical celebrations.

Before you gather the liturgy team, be sure to have all the materials you might need. For example, lectionary and sacramentary, Bible, Bible commentary(s), hymnals or other musical resources (tapes of the hymns), environment ideas, prayer and drama resources, popular music which might be used, audiovisual ideas and resources, art ideas and resources.

A PROCESS FOR PREPARING
LITURGICAL CELEBRATIONS

STEP ONE: GATHER THE GROUP AND PRAY TOGETHER
STEP TWO: REFLECTION ON THE THEME OF THE CELEBRATION

Option 1: Beginning with the Scriptures

When preparing a liturgical celebration for Sunday or a Church feast day be sure to begin with the Scripture readings chosen by the Church. Too often liturgy planners overlook the readings of the day for "specially selected" readings that will be "appropriate" for the young people. The following processes can assist you in helping young people reflect on the message of the Scripture readings and apply that message to their lives and to the process of preparing the liturgical celebration.

Both processes enable young people to name the theme of the celebration by reflection on the Scriptures. (Be sure to review Chapter 8A, "Guidelines for Reading Scripture" by Kathleen Fischer before you before the Scripture reflection process.)

There are four essential elements for understanding the readings of the liturgy:

Element 1: Consider the tone of the liturgical season. How does the liturgy of this Sunday or feast day fit within the movement of the liturgical year?

Element 2: Pick out the themes of each reading using a process of scripture reflection (see below). Write them down.

Element 3: Identify the overall message of the readings taken as whole. Note how they fit the movement of the liturgical season.

Element 4: Having identified the themes, begin to prepare the celebration.

Here is the first process for reflecting on the Scripture readings selected by the Church for the celebration:

1. *Read the Scriptures aloud (reading by reading).*
2. *Pause for silence after each reading. (Background music can help set a tone for reflection.)*
3. *Summarize the historical and cultural background for each reading using a good biblical commentary.*
4. *Provide quiet time for reflection on each commentary. (Background music can help set a tone for reflection.)*
5. *Invite group members to share the response to the scripture readings. Have each person comment on the readings by way of their reflections on the possible meaning for their lives.*

Here is a second process for reflecting on the Scripture readings that utilizes the imagination and the senses. By inviting the group members to place themselves in the Scripture story or event, it is possible to experience another dimension of Jesus' word. This process works very well with Gospel passages, Old Testament stories, and narrative passages in the epistles. It will not work well with passages taken from the Wisdom literature, the theological reflection passages of the epistles or any section of the Scripture which does not have a context which can be approached through the senses.

The group may wish to share at each level of the process. It is important that sufficient time is taken to develop steps one and two because they are the foundation upon which steps three and four are built. If sufficient time is not given to these steps, there will be insufficient data upon which to base the final step.

1. Listen carefully to the Scripture story. Carefully note all the concrete facts. For example: Where was Jesus? Whom was he with? To whom was he speaking? What was the occasion? (If it is not a Gospel story, the insert the appropriate character.)
2. Having noted the details of the episode, now reflect upon the passage a second time. Concentrate upon imagining the passage through your senses. For example: What do you see? What do you hear? What do you taste, smell? What do you experience in your sense of touch? What is the overall feeling that you identify in this passage?

3. Choose a person in this Scripture passage who fits your sense of your self.
   For example: With whom do you identify? What about this person is like
   you? How is their relationship to Jesus like that of yourself? What do they
   seek from the Lord Jesus that is like what you seek from the Lord? How does
   Jesus relate to them? How does this meeting change them? (In the Hebrew
   Scriptures use Yahweh or Lord instead of Jesus.)

4. After completing steps one through three, take a few moments to identify
   what you feel the Lord is saying to you, to us, in this passage. (In the Hebrew
   Scriptures use Yahweh or Lord instead of Jesus.) For example: What is the
   message for us? What is the passage calling us to in our lives? How can we
   respond to the call of this Scripture passage? (These questions are answered
   first on a personal level then on a group/community level.)

Option 2: Beginning with Experience

When preparing a liturgical celebration around a particular experience or event,
you will need to engage the group members in reflecting on that experience and
from that reflection process to determine the Scripture readings. Instead of
beginning with the theme (as chosen by the adults or by one or two group
members), it is recommended that you involve the young people in reflecting on
the experience or event and from that process determine a theme which names
what the group has heard and discovered. Then, appropriate Scripture readings can
be selected which will celebrate the theme and deepen the experience of the theme.
The following process can assist you in helping young people reflect on an
experience, name a theme, and then select Scripture readings.

1. *What are we celebrating or commemorating? Pray and reflect upon the
   experience to be celebrated. (Background music can help set a tone for
   reflection.)*

2. *Invite each person to share his or her personal experiences or story. Have
   each person comment on the meaning of the experience for his or her life.*

3. *As a group, give a name which would describe what has been heard and
   discovered. By naming the experience, the group will develop a theme.*

4. *Using the theme, select Scripture readings which celebrate and deepen the
   experience. A Bible concordance and scripture commentaries can assist you
   select appropriate readings.*

5: *Having identified the theme and readings, begin to prepare the celebration.*

STEP THREE: CHARACTER OF THE WORSHIPPING COMMUNITY

Consider the following elements in describing the particular worshipping
community:

1. *Who is the community celebrating? Is it a small group of youth or a retreat
   group or a parish community liturgy?*

2. *What matches the needs of the worshipping community?*

3. *What can be done to help the (young) people feel a high degree of
   participation in the liturgical celebration?*

4. *What ministerial roles will be needed?*

STEP FOUR: PREPARING THE ELEMENTS OF THE CELEBRATION

In Step Four you will be answering the following two questions, "How can we help people experience and understand what we are celebrating or commemorating?" and "In what ways will people participate in the liturgical celebration?' To assist you in answering these questions, here are several elements of liturgical celebrations that you can integrate into your celebration. As you select elements for your celebration be sure to be aware of inclusive language, appropriate images of God, and cultural pluralism. Be sure to utilize symbols that relate to the experiences of the people who are celebrating. To summarize all of your work, use the Liturgical Proposal Worksheet at the end of this chapter.

Environment (Art, Decor): In setting the environment for liturgy consider the following: seasons of the church year, seasons of the calendar year, current events, spirit of the assembling, and physical environment. The physical surroundings for worship include areas of the *worship space* (entryway, baptismal area, seating for assembly, seating of the ministers, presider's chair, altar, lectern), *objects* (processional cross, candlesticks and candles, books, vestments, vessels, images [tapestries, sculpture, cloth hangings, paintings)] audiovisuals), *objects particular to a season* (baptism font, Easter candle, advent wreath), and *lighting and color.*

Music: Selecting liturgical music which is reflective of the theme and based on the known repertoire of the musicians. Selecting popular music, appropriate to the theme and celebration, which can be sung or used as a reflection or used to accompany an audiovisual experience. Music selection should include both the ordinary parts of the liturgy, as well as the processional songs.Tom Tomaszek identifies the following simple criteria for choosing songs for worship:

* *Does it say what we want to sing?*
* *Will it help the whole assembly to pray?*
* *Is this song singable by a large group? (range, repetition, melody)*
* *Does the song fit this liturgical situation? (sound, style, rhythm)*
* *Does the song fit the rest of our liturgical setting and plan?*

Tom Conry offers the following questions to help select music for liturgy:

Is it coherent? The text should do something more than rhyme. It should convey a harmony of belief and maintain a common vector with the rest of your program.

Is it intimate? Do we say things to one another about how we really feel, our highest hopes, our most profound doubts, our darkest fears? Are we able to say things in the assembly that would be difficult to say elsewhere, making that space a liberating one?

Is it just? Does the text contain sexist or otherwise chauvinistic references? Does it turn our attention to the real problems of injustice and selfishness, reminding us of our societal obligations?

Is it challenging? Musically, is the melody strong and beautiful, or merely trite? Textually, does it call us to consider new ideas, to re-examine our lives? It is about conversion?

Is it truthful? Does it really convey our set of beliefs? Is it about the God we believe in? Or is it unclear, laden with ambiguous and obscure imagery and outdated theology? Worse yet, does it disseminate out-and-out lies?

Is it rooted in the community? Does it identify us in relation to God and one another? Does it name us really as we are or would like to be? Or is it full of "God-talk," that second language of cliches and well-worn phrases that focuses somewhere "out there" and keeps God distant and unreal? (Conry 83-84)

Movement, Gesture, Drama: Deciding on utilizing movement and gesture in the liturgy through interpretive dance, processional activity, prayer gestures or positions. Utilizing drama (mime or skits) to portray and proclaim the Scriptures. (Consult Chapter 9B, "Liturgical Drama," by Michael Moynahan for excellent ideas on using drama in the liturgy.)

Audiovisual: Researching and/or creating a slide show, video or film to be used in the liturgical celebration.

Texts: Selecting and/or creating the call to worship, penitential rite, general intercessions (introduction, petitions, conclusion), and prayers.

If you are preparing the liturgy with a group, you can divide the members into a number of small work groups. There are at least five subgroup possibilities: environment (art, decor), music, movement/gesture/drama, audiovisual, and texts. Not all the groups are formed each time. On a given occasion, the leaders may call for three or four preparation groups from this list, and the youth choose the one they wish to join. As the available groups are listed the leader summarizes their tasks as outlined above.

While meeting, each group needs a leader and/or a resource person. The leader knows ahead of time their group assignment and as the large youth group chooses areas, they go with them. (A great opportunity for peer ministry.) While these subgroups are meeting, one person (preferably the one who will preside) moves from group to group making suggestions that will tie together the various efforts.

The various elements can be integrated into a worship experience by either assigning a small group to care for that task or asking each subgroup to report back to the large group and have the presider coordinate the input and integrate it into the worship experience. (The goal is an integrated not patchwork experience.)

STEP FIVE: ASSIGNING RESPONSIBILITIES

The next phase of preparation is translating all the discussions and plans into action. Reserve the last ten to fifteen minutes of any liturgy preparation team meeting to assigning responsibilities and writing out what each person has agreed to accomplish prior to the liturgical event. Here's a simplified list of questions which may be of assistance:

1. *Who's responsible for coordinating all aspects of this liturgy?*
2. *Who will contact the presider or homilist (in the case when that individual is not present for this meeting)?*
3. *Who will make arrangements for the use of the worship space, either*

scheduling or requesting necessary permissions?

4. *Who is responsible for hospitality or other social activities surrounding the liturgy?*
5. *Who will request the necessary copyright permissions?*
6. *Who will prepare the Order of Worship (if one is being used)?*
7. *Who will coordinate the music or choir, or be a contact to the music director?*
8. *Who is responsible for stipends and other expenses?*
9. *Who will make plans for any needed announcements or publicity about the event?*
10. *When will we meet to evaluate the liturgical event?*
11. *Who will serve in the various liturgical ministry roles: Music Ministers, Eucharistic Ministers, Ministers of Hospitality, Ministers of the Word?*

Especially when youth are involved in these preparations for the first time, make sure that they have the necessary information to carry out the tasks they are assigned. If numbers allow, designate two or more youth to work together on a task, perhaps pairing an older youth with one who is less experienced in these matters.

STEP SIX: EVALUATION

In addition to the insights and suggestions offered by Tom Tomaszek in Chapter 7 and Gilbert Ostdiek in Chapter 7 for evaluation of liturgical celebrations, here are several questions, adapted from *Groundwork: Planning Liturgical Seasons*, that can guide your evaluation process:

Overall

1. Did the spirit of the theme (or season) permeate the liturgical celebration? Consider the art, ritual, music, prayer texts, homilies, etc.
2. What was the response of the assembly? Anything observable? Comments?

Environment and Art

1. In what ways did the art and environment reflect or create the mood?
2. What invited prayer? What distracted from prayer?
3. Were objects well crafted?

Ritual Movement

1. Were the rituals well carried out by the ministers and the assembly alike?
2. Did any ritual dominate attention or overshadow more important actions of the Mass?

Music

1. Did the music reflect or create the mood of the season?
2. Was the music well fit to the ritual?
3. Were the texts appropriate to the theme?
4. Was the music well performed?
5. How well did the assembly participate?

Prayer Texts

1. Were the prayer texts well suited to the theme and liturgy?
2. Were they spoken well? Were they easily understood?

Recommendations
1. Is there anything that you would like to see improved upon?
2. Is there anything you think should not be done again?

WORKS CITED

Conry. Tom. "Choosing Music: No Small Task." *Pastoral Music in Practice.* Edited by Virgil Funk and Gabe Huck. Washington, DC: Pastoral Chicago: Liturgy Training Publications, 1986.

LITURGICAL PROPOSAL

Date: _____ Time: _____ Location: _____

FEAST OR SPECIAL OCCASION: _____

THEME: _____

LITURGICAL MINISTERS:
    Presider: _____
    Hospitality Ministers: _____
    Ministers of the Word: _____
    Music Ministers: _____
    Eucharistic Ministers: _____
    Other Ministers: _____

ENVIRONMENT AND ART: _____
_____
_____
_____
_____
_____
_____

RITUAL MOVEMENT AND GESTURE: _____
_____
_____
_____
_____
_____
_____

MUSIC:
    Introductory Rites:
        Gathering _____
        Penitential rite_____
        Other _____

    Liturgy of the Word:
        Responsorial psalm_____
        Gospel acclamation _____
        Other _____

    Preparation of the Altar: _____

    Liturgy of the Eucharist:
        Acclamations _____
        Lamb of God_____
        Communion _____

    Departure: _____

TEXTS:
    Introductory Rites: _____
_____

    General Intercessions: _____
_____

    Eucharistic Prayer:_____
_____

    Communion Rite:_____
_____

    Dismissal: _____
_____

Pages 140-141 may be duplicated for non-commerical educational purposes.

Chapter 10

An Overview of the Communal Rites of Penance

By Edward Foley, OFM Cap.

The introduction to the *Rite of Penance* reminds us that reconciliation was foundational to the ministry of Jesus Christ and his Church (nos. 1-2). It was through Jesus' life, death, and resurrection that the world was reconciled to God. In the spirit of this same Jesus Christ the Church has been empowered to call all to conversion and show the victory of Christ over sin.

This reconciling ministry has assumed a myriad of shapes and forms over the centuries, and manifold are the ways believers have been invited into Christ's victory over sin. Chief among these are certain sacraments of the Church. It is first in Baptism that we are "freed from all sin, given ... a new birth by water and the Holy Spirit, and welcomed ... into his holy people."[1] In the Eucharist we are invited to share the gifts of the new covenant, poured out for us so that sins may be forgiven. In the sacrament of Penance our hearts are cleansed and our sins forgiven, that we might "proclaim the mighty acts of God who has called [us] out of darkness into the splendor of his light." (no. 62) Finally, the Anointing of the Sick "provides the sick person with the forgiveness of sins and the completion of Christian penance." *(Rite of Anointing* no. 6)

We will now consider the structure and content of the Rite for Reconciliation of Several Penitents with Individual Confession and Absolution (Rite II), and the Rite for Reconciliation of Several Penitents with General Confession and Absolution (Rite III). Our concern is to ascertain some of the strengths and weaknesses of these rites in light of the broad context discussed about communal rites of penance, which we will attempt to incorporate into the three scenarios at the end of this paper.

In outline form we can see a fundamental similarity between these two rites: (See Page 143)

There are numerous facets of these rites which have been praised since their appearance in 1973. First among these is the new ecclesial emphasis which reconciliation receives, as well as the clear social emphasis of these rites. Here, we are

RITE II	RITE III
Introductory rites	Introductory Rites
song	song
greeting	greeting
opening prayer	opening prayer
Celebration of the Word	Celebration of the Word
reading	reading
response	response
second reading	second reading
Gospel acclamation	Gospel acclamation
Gospel	Gospel
homily	homily
	Instruction
Examination of Conscience	Examination of Conscience
Rite of Reconciliation	Rite of Reconciliation
general confession	general confession
individual	general absolution
	proclamation of praise
confession/absolution	
proclamation of praise	
prayer of thanksgiving	
Concluding rites	Concluding rites

dramatically reminded that sin is not merely a private failing, but a collective experience which affects the entire Body of Christ. The rites attend to Scripture, returning the Word to its proper place in the sacrament. It is precisely through the Word that God calls us to repentance and leads us to a true conversion of heart. (no. 24) Finally, the development of Rite III and the introduction of general absolution is a most important innovation, with wide pastoral possibilities. The reform is not so much a passage from one rite to another, as a transformation of a mentality and style of celebration, ultimately moving from a reform of rites to a reform of life. (Sottocornola 89-136)

Given these positive aspects of Rites II and III, there are also substantial theological-liturgical problems with these sacramental forms. Specifically speaking of Rite II, William Marrevee has noted that, though there is a concern to blend personal and communal dimensions in the rite, the elements surrounding individual confession and absolution are rather circumstantial. (Marrevee 130) Concerning Rite III, Marrevee underlines as problematic the exceptional nature of general absolution. Noting that the *Rite of Penance* makes it clear that individual confession and absolution are the norm, he believes that the basic preoccupation of Rite III (like Rite II) is individual confession and absolution.

As both rites can be criticized for their emphasis on individual confession and absolution, so could both rites be criticized for their structural monotony and verbosity. Structurally, these two rites (as well as Rite I) are virtually identical.

Moreover, the fundamental outline for Rites II and III is the same as the Eucharist: with confession and absolution replacing the eucharistic prayer and communion rite. The overuse of this structure is certainly problematic. Furthermore, these rites are long on text but short on symbolic action. Yet the symbolic act is as fundamental to the experience of reconciliation as the taking, blessing, breaking and giving of bread and wine are to Eucharist.

Finally, at the heart of the criticism, there is a deep concern these rites do not attend to the process of reconciliation, which by definition takes place over time. As James Dallen has summarized, this view of penance as a process extending over time was at least implicit in the contemporary theology during the period of preparation for the new Rite of Penance. (Dallen 202-221) Since the appearance of the Rite, this awareness has grown explicit. (Bernardin 41-44) Like the Rite of Christian Initiation of Adults, which understands initiation as a gradual incorporation into the community punctuated by rites, so is true reconciliation a gradual reincorporation into the same community, requiring the same ritual punctuation.

PRINCIPLES FOR COMMUNAL RITES OF PENANCE

Given our summary discussions of the wider context of the Rite of Penance, as well as the specific critique of Rites II and III, we are now in a position to extract a few principles about the rites which can inform our preparation. Following the statement and explanation of these principles, we will offer three variant examples of how they might be applied.

Our discussion of the Church's rich and varied penitential vocabulary suggests our first principle: *the sacramental forms found in the Rite of Penance cannot bear the weight of the entire reconciliation process.* Just as the Eucharist cannot be the only rite in our liturgical vocabulary for giving thanks and constituting ourselves as the living Body of Christ, so we cannot expect the various forms in the Rite of Penance to be our only ritual encounters in forgiveness. It is true, to continue the analogy, that the eucharistic liturgy is the focal way in which we are constituted as the Body of Christ, and enjoys a clear primacy in this regard. *(Constitution on the Sacred Liturgy* no. 10) The eucharistic liturgy, however, cannot be the only worship experience which enables this. Such limitation does not do justice either to the rich liturgical and theological traditions of the Church - or the people's real need for a wide range of liturgical experiences which will allow them to enter the Eucharist more completely.[2] In the same way, though the various "sacramental" forms in the Rite of Penance are focal and assume a clear primacy in the Church's penitential vocabulary, they cannot be the only such moments and means. To confine forgiveness to these three rites is to ignore the good wisdom of the ages and the real need of the faithful.

A second principle flows from the first. Since the various "sacramental" forms in the Rite of Penance cannot bear the weight of every need, then *we need to integrate other penitential practices into the given sacramental forms of reconciliation.* It is important to encourage a wide range of traditional practices such as works of charity, mutual forgiveness, fasting, and almsgiving. Given the special place, however, which the formal rites of penance hold - especially as they culminate in absolution - it seems essential to integrate these with the ongoing practices of the faithful. This integration not only validates normal penitential practices as an integral part of the reconciliation process, but it also serves to play down the almost magical emphasis given to absolution.

Third, we have recognized that there are numerous needs, various kinds of alienation, and many expectations for the rite of penance. This suggests that *there should be flexibility in the rites of reconciliation, and the possibility for particularizing the rites to suit various expectations and needs.* This does not necessarily imply that every form of reconciliation must be able to respond to every penitential need. It is quite possible, instead, that some forms could be structured to respond to specific kinds of alienation and sin. The principle does suggest, however, that adaptability of the rites to the particular needs of each penitent or group of penitents is a value.

Fourth, our critique of Rites II and III surfaced the realization that reconciliation is not fundamentally a verbal experience. It is the enacted ritual and the embodied embrace of the community which best articulates and effects reincorporation. Consequently, *rites of reconciliation need to be marked by rich symbolic action, which must be integral to the ritual.*

Finally, our summary of the strengths and weaknesses of the current rites also reminded us that *reconciliation is fundamentally a process of reincorporation into the Body of Christ.* Two elements seem essential here. First, just as sin alienates us from God, other, and self, so does reconciliation strengthen and reestablish this tripartite bond. Second, such reincorporation takes time. It is not a moment event, though it might be culminated in a powerful ritual moment. Consequently, the rites which serve this reincorporation must respect both the process and the ecclesial dimension of reconciliation.

APPLICATIONS

We now arrive at the final stage of application. In a sense, this is the most artificial part of our discussion, because reader and author share no real community experience in which to ground these pastoral suggestions. What we offer, therefore, should be taken as theoretical scenarios which cannot be indiscriminately imposed upon a community. These "models" must, instead, be adapted to local needs, traditions and capacities. The three following scenarios will address different pastoral situations. Needless to say, there are many more. Hopefully these samples will indicate some of the possibilities for adapting Rites II and III.

SCENARIO I: A WEEKEND RETREAT

A weekend retreat holds great potential for crafting a reconciliation service which would respect the diverse needs of the individuals and the process of the Rite. This could especially be true if the celebration focused on a specific kind of alienation or brokenness like divorce or chemical dependency. In this Friday evening to Sunday afternoon experience, a complete process of reconciliation is not possible. The weekend could be so structured, however, so that the process might begin or be strengthened; it would then need to be continued after the weekend was over.

One reason the weekend retreat offers such rich possibilities is because of its natural movement from the day of the cross (Friday) to the day of resurrection (Sunday). This cyclic progression is a weekly icon for the Good Friday to Easter Sunday journey. Its potential in reconciliation should be overlooked. Furthermore, Sunday as the primordial day for Eucharist, which is the ritual finale to authentic reincorporation, offers rich direction to the entire process.

It would be necessary in this scenario to prepare the participants before their arrival. To be led in an intense process of reconciliation requires preparation. A retreat so envisioned would not only have to be appropriately advertised (for example, "A Journey in Forgiveness"), but participants would also need to come prepared to face their own alienation or brokenness.

As a variation on Rite II, the ritual structure for the three days could entail the following components:

1. *gathering in hope, and acknowledgement of alienation and/or sinfulness (Friday evening);*
2. *proclamation of God's mercy and invitation, in the Word (Friday evening);*
3. *reflection on our common holiness and need for purification (Saturday morning);*
4. *individual sharing with presbyter, retreat staff, spouse, friend, etc., on one's personal alienation or sin (Saturday afternoon);*
5. *communal gathering, reiteration of the Word, space for individual sharing of reflections, prayer, or experiences (Saturday evening);*
6. *prayer service, incorporating individual gestures of return, laying on of hands, and the Church's declaration of forgiveness (Saturday night);*
7. *Eucharist (Sunday morning);*
8. *festive meal (Sunday noon);*
9. *mystagogia on the reconciliation encountered, and the journey yet ahead (Sunday afternoon).*

Recalling our principles, this scenario does not put all the emphasis on "absolution," but gives equal weight to elements of Word, sharing, and reflection, with pride of place given to Eucharist. There could be great flexibility in the scenario, as for example, in the choice of presbyter, retreat staff, or other in the sharing of personal alienation or sin. Integration of the various elements could be achieved not only by the prepared reflections by the retreat staff which naturally accompany such a weekend, but also by echoing previous ritual elements in each succeeding step, or by a single continuous word, symbol, or song throughout the weekend. This scenario also acknowledges that reconciliation is a journey over time, for which the weekend serves as a paradigm. Two of the challenges of this model are calling the participants to properly prepare for the weekend, and to continue the reincorporation after the retreat is over.

SCENARIO II: A SINGLE PARISH GATHERING IN ADVENT

Often the local community can only gather a single time for a celebration of penance. It is yet possible, however, to prepare this single gathering so that it respects the process of reconciliation. Preparation is again an essential component. It is important to know what Scriptures will be proclaimed, the focus of the homily, and whatever symbolic gesture or music will be employed. These elements, well planned in advance, will serve both the preparation for the gathering and the actual ritual.

The service would need to be contextualized in the wider movement of the Church year. This will allow integration of the basic motifs and symbols which give direction to the whole of a season's worship into the reconciliation service. During Advent, for example, the season turns on the image of solstice, and the triumph of Jesus the light over all darkness. This motif could find resonance in a journey to reconciliation which invites us to consider where we are the light of Christ, or how we cast shadows on the message of the Gospel.

The Advent wreath, potentially present in the church and in the home, could serve as a symbolic focus for the seasonal journey. During the entrance rites for the First Sunday of Advent the wreath could be blessed with a text which recalls our baptismal commitment to walk as children of the light. This text could be related to prayer for ("Lord, have") mercy for the times as individuals and community we have chosen the darkness, for example,

> Blessed are you, Wisdom of the ages, for your goodness has revealed itself from the dawn of time and your salvation is made known in Jesus the Christ.
> Bless us in this season of waning light. Increase our longing for your son and our willingness to grow in his love.
> As we light this candle [these candles] in expectation of his final return,
> Give us strength to shun the darkness, and witness to your glory,
> That the dawn of his presence may find us rejoicing in his word and welcoming his truth.
> We ask this in the name of Jesus the Lord.

This same lighting of the wreath could be done in each household of the community. In preparation for the daily lighting of the wreath, members of each household could be invited to share what area of their life they wish to be enlightened. A familiar song like "O Come, O Come Emmanuel," with its textual images of ransom and liberation could accompany both the eucharistic entrance rites and the family wreath lighting.

Three weeks of light and blessing, confessing and family penitential practices could punctuate this special season of charity and almsgiving. These would also prepare for the communal service of reconciliation, which could take the following shape:

1. *Begin with the same opening rituals around the wreath, employing variations on the same musical setting and a variation on the same opening prayer;*
2. *proclaim the Word of promise in Christ who is the light to the nations;*
3. *invite two or three individuals, or members of a single household, to speak of their Advent reflections or journey toward the light;*

4. *confess publicly our individual and communal failure to prepare the way of the Lord;*
5. *offer general absolution;*
6. *as a symbol of reincorporation and recommitment, light candles off the Advent wreath and share with all members of the community while singing "O Come, O Come Emmanuel";*
7. *dismissal.*

It is also possible to integrate a parish's option for the poor into this reconciliation journey. Households could be invited to share one simple meal each week, which would serve as a special focus of prayer and sharing. The food that they would normally eat, or expenditures for that food could be give over to the poor. Some kind of food or monetary collection could be taken from the people as they enter the church for the reconciliation service.

It is further possible to extend the ritual journey beyond the Advent season, by using the lighting of candles as an opening rite during the Christmas season. Therein recall the baptismal commitment made to Christ who is the never-fading light, and invite the community to recommit itself to the mission of incarnating this same Christ into the world.

The possibilities are endless; the task is to rely on the seasonal movements in prayer, symbol, and activity, and choreograph them into a coherent ritual movement which encourages a process of reconciliation, and integrates it with life and mission.

SCENARIO III: MULTIPLE PARISH GATHERINGS DURING LENT

A final scenario for communal reconciliation is composed of multiple gatherings of the community during the premier season of purification and enlightenment, Lent. The ritual hinge for these gatherings could be the three scrutinies for the baptismal elect, which occur on the Third, Fourth, and Fifth Sundays of Lent. These scrutinies have a twofold purpose, "revealing anything that is weak, defective, or sinful in the hearts of the elect, so that it may be healed, and revealing what is upright, strong and holy, so that it may be strengthened." (RCIA, no. 25.1) This dual purpose is quite applicable to the post-baptismal reconciliation process. Whether or not a community has candidates for Easter initiation, the rehearsal of these scrutinies during Lent could be a valuable ritual guide for the entire community.

The "rehearsal" of each scrutiny could take place on a weeknight before the designated Sunday. The scrutiny which normally occurs on the Third Sunday of Lent, for example, would serve as the basis of a penance service on Wednesday of the second week. The structure of this service could be:

1. *gathering;*
2. *proclamation of the Gospel for the coming Sunday;*
3. *catechesis on the journey to baptismal recommitment during Lent, and the role of the scrutinies in that journey;*
4. *prayer for the community, adapted from the scrutiny's prayer for the elect; (RCIA, no. 163)*

5. *prayer of exorcism, adapted from the exorcism prayer in the scrutiny;*
   ((RCIA, no. 164)
6. *a prayer of blessing;*
7. *end of communal ritual, and opportunity for individual prayer with parish*
   staff, with options of private confession, anointing (adapted from
   catechumenal anointings), laying on of hands, etc.;
8. *fellowship.*

Three such services during the second, third, and fourth weeks of Lent could prepare the community for the scrutinies in the Sunday assembly, encourage a communal awareness of the post-baptismal Lenten journey, and invite people into a process of reconciliation. Absolution, at least in its communal form, should be postponed until Wednesday of the firth week.[3] This service could revolve around the presentation of the profession of faith or the Lord's Prayer, which are also proper to the journey towards Easter initiation. (RCIA, nos. 183-193) Employing basically the same structure of the three previous weeks, this final reconciliation service would end with general absolution, and singing the Lord's Prayer as a common penance.

The proclamation of forgiveness (absolution) should not, however, be presented as the culmination of the Lenten journey. Every effort should be made to lead people into the Triduum, which is the ultimate celebration of the reincorporation of sinners (Thursday), the encounter with the crucified one poured out for us (Friday), and the final victory over sin (Easter Vigil).

Ritually these individual segments are easily connected through the use of common symbols, e.g., a continuous piece of music. The weekly reiteration at the Wednesday services and through the Triduum of a song like "We Remember" jogs the memory, invites connections, and leads to closure.[4] Parishes which are used to a Lenten series or mission could invite a special preacher to these four Wednesday evenings for continuous catechesis on the season's rituals. Whatever the traditional strengths of a parish community during this Lenten season, they should be respected and integrated into this process of reconciliation.

CONCLUSION

As cautioned in the beginning, authentic liturgical preparation is not a scramble for the newest technique or structural innovation. Rather, it is acknowledging the relationship of worship which exists in Godself, and enabling believers to encounter the same. Adapting the communal rites of penance requires no less. Respect for individual needs in this encounter is paramount. It is in the context of this respect, and in view of the rich and varied tradition of the Church, that our reconciling ministry must continue.

END NOTES

[1] Optional prayer for anointing after baptism, *Rite of Christian Initiation of Adults* (RCIA), no. 224. This and all subsequent quotations of the rites are taken from *The Rites of the Catholic Church* (New York: Pueblo, 1976).

[2] The *Directory for Masses with Children* makes this clear when discussing the introduction of children to the Eucharist (nos. 8-15). I would suggest that most of the principles articulated in this document are applicable to adults as well.

[3] People experiencing "individual confession" should also be encouraged to postpone absolution until this final service, though absolution cannot be denied them if they so desire it.

[4] "We Remember" from the collection *With Open Hands* by Marty Haugen (Chicago: G.I.A., 1981).

WORKS CITED

Bernardin, Joseph Cardinal. "Proposal for a New Rite of Penance." *Synod of Bishops, 1983, Penance and Reconciliation.*

Dallen, James. "A Decade of Discussion on the Reform of Penance, 1963-1973: Theological Analysis and Critique." S.T.D. Diss. Catholic U of America, 1976.

Introduction to the Rite of Anointing and Pastoral Care of the Sick. The Rites of the Catholic Church. New York: Pueblo, 1976.

Marrevee, William. "The New 'Order of Penance' - Is It Adequate?" *Eglise et Theologie* 7 (1976): 130.

"Pastoral Norms" 16 June 1972, Congregation for the Doctrine of the Faith. *Documents on the Liturgy 1963-1979.* Collegeville: Liturgical, 1982.

Sottocornola, Franco. "Les nouveaux rites de la penitence: comentaire." *Questions Liturgiques* 45 (1974): 89-136.

Chapter 11

Guide for Planning Community Reconciliation Celebrations

The following guide is meant to integrate many of the insights and elements of reconciliation services into an outline that you can use in preparing a a variety of reconciliation services. This guide can be used to prepare a communal celebration of the Sacrament of Reconciliation or a non-sacramental reconciliation experiences. Prior to using this guide, please review Chapter 10 - "An Overview of the Communal Rites of Penance" and Chapter 8 - "Elements for Preparing Liturgical Celebrations." Be sure to consult the resource guide in Chapter 12 for materials to assist you in preparing the celebration. Before you gather prepare the service, be sure to have all the materials you might need. For example, the *Rite of Penance*, Bible, Bible commentary(s), hymnals or other musical resources (tapes of the hymns), environment ideas, prayer and drama resources, popular music which might be used, audiovisual ideas and resources, art ideas and resources.

OVERVIEW

Communal reconciliation services seek to enable the community gathered and the individuals who make it up to: a) express sorrow for sinfulness and b) experience the reconciling power of the Lord in their midst. There are special "moments" in this rite:

 a. *the experience of being called and gathered by the Lord.*
 b. *the experience of hearing the Good News of the Lord: how God loves us so deeply in Christ and wants us to be one with Godself.*
 c. *the recognition of the power of sin in our lives both as a group and as individuals.*
 d. *the specific recognition of what in my life keeps me from living the Gospel as I know I ought.*
 e. *the confession of sinfulness in the light of God's grace and God's call to conversion.*
 f. *the experience of being reconciled by the Lord through the ministry of the priest and through the prayerful support of the assembly.*
 g. *joyful thanksgiving to the Lord and a desire to live the Gospel life.*

ELEMENTS OF RECONCILIATION CELEBRATIONS

Symbols: When preparing a reconciliation service be sure to use symbols that work for the community gathered. For example: incense rising at moments of communal prayer, confession, thanksgiving; candles being lighted by those who have just confessed, bathing the room in Christ's light; hands being anointed with oil as part of the absolution or as part of a communal reconciliation gesture after individual reconciliation; the sharing of the sign of peace. Simplicity in sign and gesture is desired.

Environment: The climate of the place for celebration should be one of warmth, reflection, and quiet. The setting should help the participant to be stilled and quiet and able to come in touch with their own brokenness and need for healing.

Gathering Song: A gathering song emphasizing either the theme of unity or healing would be most appropriate. It is also appropriate to use songs which emphasize the mercy of God, thankfulness for God's saving love or praise for what God has done for us.

Introduction: A few words could be shared on the purpose of coming together as a people to seek forgiveness. It should include the concept that we need forgiveness as individuals and as a community.

Prayer of Petition: It is sometimes helpful to have a litany of forgiveness at this time. The litany can include invocations reflecting on the state of the world, the reality of human sinfulness or on our personal sinfulness.

Readings: A characteristic of communal reconciliation services is the role of the Word. It is important to listen to the message of forgiveness found in the Scriptures as well as to its call to conversion of heart. You might have two Scripture readings connected by a psalm or you might wish to have three readings and include a contemporary one. Readings ought to reflect both the structure of the rite and the liturgical season. The selections taken as a whole should include a focus on a) God's love and mercy in Christ, and b) call to conversion from our sinfulness. Both elements are important; both must be kept in balance.

Response: The response to the Word might take the form of a homily, a shared reflection among the group, a movie, an activity or experience which helps the participants to internalize the message of the Scriptures and move to inner conversion of heart.

Invitation to Reconciliation: All are invited to seek healing from the Lord and from each other.

Examination of Life: Time should be given for participants to reflect upon the manner in which they are living out their response to Jesus. In what ways have they been faithful/unfaithful...in what ways have we, as a group, failed to witness to the Gospel? The examination should not be overly negative but should be a way of inviting one to conversion.

Request for Forgiveness: In a sacramental reconciliation rite, this would be the time for sacramental confession. Those who wish to receive the sacrament would approach the confessor and ask forgiveness. Usually this is very brief and counseling is not done in this context. During the time of sacramental confession, it is appropriate for the whole group to pray and sing as long as it does not hinder the confessor's ability to hear those who are receiving the sacrament. Penance and absolution are given to those who have confessed and a sign of reconciliation is given. The Greeting of Peace is most appropriate at this point.

In non-sacramental reconciliation services, the participants would indicate by some sign that they which God's forgiveness but should be aware that this is not a sacramental celebration.

Closing Song: This song should have the tone of thanksgiving and praise.

RITE OF PENANCE - FORM II

The following is a guide for preparing communal reconciliation services with individual confession and absolution.

Entrance Rites

    Opening Song, Greeting, Prayer: ....called and gathered in the Lord

    Celebration of the Word of God: ....hearing good news
    Reading: ....God's love for us
    Response (psalm/song): ....our awareness of sin
    Reading (optional): ....our awareness of sin
    Gospel-Homily: ....call to conversion
    Examination of Conscience: ....call to conversion

Rite of Reconciliation

    General Confession
    (prayer or litany and Lord's Prayer): ....expression of sorrow
    Individual Confession
        & Reconciliation,
    Communal Praise,
    Thanksgiving
    (song, prayer, gesture): ....personal encounter, communion

Closing Rites

    Blessing and Dismissal: ....sending into the world

Chapter 12

A Resource Guide for Preparing Liturgical Celebrations

CHURCH DOCUMENTS

The Liturgy Documents — A Parish Resource. Chicago: Liturgy Training, 1980.
(includes *Directory for Masses with Children, Music in Catholic Worship,* and
Environment and Art in Catholic Worship).
The Rites of the Catholic Church. New York: Pueblo, 1976. (includes the *Rite of Penance*).

THEOLOGY OF WORSHIP

Boff, Leonardo. *Sacraments of Life, Life of the Sacraments.* Washington, DC: Pastoral, 1987.
Collins, Mary. *Worship: Renewal to Practice.* Washington, D.C.: Pastoral, 1987.
Collins, Patrick. *More Than Meets The Eye: Ritual and Parish Liturgy.* New York: Paulist, 1983.
Cooke, Bernard. *Sacraments and Sacramentality.* Mystic: Twenty-Third, 1983.
Coyle, Tom. *This is Our Mass,* Rev. ed. Mystic: Twenty-Third, 1989.
Dallen, James. *Gathering for Eucharist: A Theology of Sunday Eucharist.* Old Hickory: Pastoral Arts, 1973.
Downey, Michael. *Clothed in Christ: The Sacraments and Christian Living.* New York: Crossroad, 1987.
Empereur, James. *Worship: Exploring the Sacred.* Washington, DC: Pastoral, 1987.
Feider, Paul. *The Sacraments: Encountering the Risen Lord.* Notre Dame: Ave Maria, 1986.
Fleming, Austin. *Preparing for Liturgy: A Theology and Spirituality.*

Washington, DC: Pastoral, 1985.

Funk, Virgil and Gabe Huck. *Pastoral Music in Practice*. Washington, DC: Pastoral Chicago: Liturgy Training, 1981.

Funk, Virgil and Gabe Huck. *Music in Catholic Worship*. Washington, DC: Pastoral, 1983.

Grosz, Edward, ed. *Liturgy and Social Justice: Celebrating Rites, Proclaiming Rites*. Collegeville: Liturgical, 1989.

Guzie, Tad. *The Book of Sacramental Basics*. New York: Paulist, 1981.

Henderson, J. Frank, et al, *Liturgy, Justice, and the Reign of God*. New York: Paulist, 1989.

Keifer, Ralph *The Mass in Time of Doubt*. Washington, DC: National Association of Pastoral Musicians, 1983.

Johnson, Lawrence, ed. *The Church Gives Thanks and Remembers*. Collegeville: Liturgical, 1984.

—————. *Called to Prayer: Liturgical Spirituality Today*. Collegeville: Liturgical, 1986.

Mick, Lawrence. *To Live as We Worship*. Collegeville: Liturgical, 1984.

—————. *Understanding the Sacraments Today*. Collegeville: Liturgical .

Searle, Mark *Liturgy Made Simple*. Collegeville: Liturgical, 1981.

Searle, Mark, ed. *Liturgy and Social Justice*. Collegeville: Liturgical, 1980.

Smolarski, SJ, Dennis. *How Not To Say Mass*. New York: Paulist, 1986.

Walsh, SS, Eugene. *The Ministry of the Celebrating Community*. Old Hickory: Pastoral Arts, 1977.

—————. *The Theology of Celebration*. Old Hickory: Pastoral Arts, 1977.

Wilde, James, ed. *At That Time: Cycles and Seasons in the Life of a Christian*. Chicago: Liturgy Training, 1989.

SACRAMENT OF RECONCILATION

Brennan, Patrick. *Penance and Reconciliation*. Chicago: Thomas More, 1986.

Cooke, Bernard. *Reconciled Sinners: Healing Human Brokenness*. Mystic: Twenty-Third, 1986.

Dallen, James. *The Reconciling Community: The Rite of Penance*. New York: Pueblo, 1986.

Donnelly, Doris. *Putting Forgiveness into Practice*. Allen: Argus, 1982.

Doran, Kevin. *More Joy in Heaven!: Confession, the Sacrament of Reconciliation*. Collegeville: Liturgical, 1988.

Henchal, Michael, ed. *Repentance and Reconciliation in the Church*. Collegeville: Liturgical, 1987.

Kennedy, Robert, ed. *Reconciliation: The Continuing Agenda*. Collegeville: Liturgical, 1987.

Mick, Lawrence. *Penance: The Once and Future Sacrament*. Collegeville: Liturgical.

O'Malley, Sarah and Robert Eimer. *Come, Let Us Celebrate: Creative Celebrations of Reconciliation*. San Jose: Resource, 1986.

PREPARATION RESOURCES

Baker, Thomas and Frank Ferrone. *Liturgy Committee Basics.* Washington, DC: Pastoral, 1989.

Brown, Grayson Warren. *Sunday Mornings: Some Reasons Why We Fail, Some Ways to Succeed.* Old Hickory: Pastoral Arts, 1980.

Cassa, Yvonne and Joanne Sanders. *Groundwork: Planning Liturgical Seasons.* Chicago: Liturgy Training, 1982.

——————. *How to Form a Parish Liturgy Board.* Chicago: Liturgy Training, 1987.

Fleming, Austin. *Preparing for Liturgy: A Theology and Spirituality.* Washington, DC: Pastoral, 1985.

Huck, Gabe, ed. *Liturgy with Style and Grace: A Basic Manual for Planners and Ministers.* Rev. ed. Chicago: Liturgy Training, 1984.

Johnson, Lawrence. *The Word and Eucharist Handbook.* San Jose: Resource, 1986.

Krier, Catherine H. *Symbols for All Seasons: Environmental Planning for Cycles A, B, & C.* San Jose: Resource, 1988.

Marchal, Michael. *Adapting the Liturgy: Creative Ideas for the Church Year.* San Jose: Resource, 1989.

Ostkiek, Gilbert. *Catechesis for Liturgy: A Program for Parish Involvement.* Washington, DC: Pastoral, 1986.

Walsh, SS, Eugene. *The Order of Mass: Guidelines.* Rev. ed. Old Hickory: Pastoral Arts, 1979.

——————. *The Ministry of the Celebrating Community.* Old Hickory: Pastoral Arts, 1977.

——————. *The Theology of Celebration.* Old Hickory: Pastoral Arts, 1977.

——————. *Practical Suggestions for Celebrating Sunday Mass.* Old Hickory: Pastoral Arts, 1978.

COMMENTARIES ON THE SUNDAY READINGS

Graham, Jacquelyn. *The Pastorals on Sundays.* Chicago: Liturgy Training, 1990. (An annual publication, correlating Catholic social teachings and the Sunday cycle of readings.)

Irwin, Kevin. *Sunday Worship: A Planning Guide to Celebration.* New York: Pueblo, 1983.

Mazar, Peter, et al. *Sourcebook for Sundays and Seasons: An Almanac of Parish Liturgy.* Chicago: Liturgy Training, 1989. (Three volumes, one for each cycle of readings and seasons. Contains resources, descriptions of and ideas for celebrating the liturgical seasons of Advent-Christmas and Lent-Triduum-Eastertime, and a calendar for every day of the year with ideas for liturgy preparation.)

Modern Liturgy Planning Guide. San Jose: Resource, 1987.

Wilde, James, et al., *At Home with the Word: 1990.* Chicago: Liturgy Training, 1989. (An annual publication with the Sunday cycle of readings and reflections.)

WORSHIP SERVICES FOR YOUTH

Benson, Dennis. *Creative Worship in Youth Ministry.* Loveland: Group, 1985.

Bailey, Betty Jane and J. Martin. *Youth Plan Worship.* New York: Pilgrim, 1987.

Black, Barbara, et al., *Pentecost, Peanuts, Popcorn, Prayer: Prayer Services for High School Students.* Villa Maria: Center for Learning, 1988.

Center for Learning. *Seasonal Liturgies.* Villa Maria: Center for Learning, 1989.

Duck, Ruth C. and Maren C. Tirabassi. *Touch Holiness: Resources for Worship.* New York: Pilgrim, 1990.

Huck, Gabe, et al. *Hymnal for Catholic Students: Leader's Manual.* Chicago: GIA and Liturgy Training, 1989. (Includes the Directory of Masses with Children, background essays, and twenty celebrations.)

McBride, William and Jeffrey Smay. *Liturgy Models.* Villa Maria: Center for Learning, 1984.

Neary, SJ, Donal. *Masses with Young People.* Rev. ed. Mystic: Twenty-Third, 1987.

Reeves, SC, John Maria and Maureen Roe, RSM. *Junior High Liturgy, Prayer, Reconciliation.* Villa Maria: Center for Learning, 1988.

Schaffran, Janet and Pat Kozak. *More Than Words: Prayer and Ritual for Inclusive Communities.* Oak Park: Meyer-Stone, 1988.

RESOURCE MATERIALS

Bethune, Ade. *Eye Contact with God through Pictures.* Kansas City: Sheed and Ward, 1986.

Center for Learning. *Images of Life Slide/Prayer Packages.* Villa Maria: Center for Learning. (Two volumes of slides, 300 slides per volume, arranged thematically. Six books of slide prayers and meditations keyed to the two volumes of slides are also available.)

Collopy, George. *It's a Banner Year!* San Jose: Resource, 1990.

——————-. *Clip Art for Bulletins and Beyond.* San Jose: Resource .

Craighead, Meinrad. *Liturgical Art.* Kansas City: Sheed and Ward, 1988.

Cunningham, Nancy Brady. *Feeding the Spirit: How to Create Your Own Ceremonial Rites, Festivals, and Celebrations.* San Jose: Resource, 1988.

DeGidio, Sandra. *Enriching Faith through Family Celebrations.* Mystic: Twenty-Third, 1989.

Gagne, Ronald, et al., *Introducing Dance in Christian Worship.* Washington, DC: Pastoral, 1984.

Henderson, J. Frank, et al., *Liturgy, Justice, and the Reign of God.* New York: Paulist, 1989.

Hock, Mary Isabelle. *Worship through the Seasons.* San Jose: Resource, 1987.

Huck, Gabe. *How Can I Keep from Singing? Thoughts about Liturgy for Musicians.* Chicago: Liturgy Training, 1989.

Huck, Gabe, et al. *Hymnal for Catholic Students: Leader's Manual.* Chicago: GIA, 1989.

Hymnal for Catholic Students. Chicago: GIA, 1989.

Kirk, Martha Ann. *Dancing with Creation — Mexican and Native American Dance in Christian Worship and Education.* San Jose: Resource, 1983.

Knuth, Jill. *Banners without Words.* San Jose: Resource.

Mapson, J. Wendell. *The Ministry of Music in the Black Church.* Valley Forge: Judson, 1984.

Morningstar, Jean. *Clip Art for Communicating the Good News.* San Jose: Resource.

Moynahan, SJ, Michael. *How the Word Became Flesh: Story Dramas for Worship and Religious Education.* San Jose: Resource, 1981.

——————. *Once Upon a Parable: Dramas for Worship and Religious Education.* New York: Paulist, 1984.

Mullaly, Larry. *The Golden Link: Gospel Playlets for Schools and Parish Liturgies.* San Jose: Resource.

Nelson, Gertrud Mueller. *To Dance with God: Family Ritual and Community Celebration.* New York: Paulist, 1986.

——————. *Clip Art for Celebrations and Service.* New York: Pueblo, 1987.

——————. *Clip Art for Feasts and Seasons.* New York: Pueblo, 1982.

Ortegel, SP, Adelaide. *Banners and Such.* San Jose: Resource.

——————, and Kent Schneider. *Light: Multimedia Techniques for Celebration.* San Jose: Resource.

Patitucci, Karen. *Three-Minute Dramas for Worship.* San Jose: Resource, 1989.

Perr, Herb. *Making Art Together Step-by-Step.* San Jose: Resource.

Schaffran, Janet and Pat Kozak. *More Than Words: Prayer and Ritual for Inclusive Communities.* Oak Park: Meyer-Stone, 1988.

Schmidt, Clemens. *Clip Art for the Liturgical Year.* Collegeville: Liturgical, 1988.

Siegel, Helen. *Clip Art for Feasts and Seasons.* New York: Pueblo, 1984.

Uhlmann, Cathy Lee and Chris. *Worship Dramas for Children and Adults.* San Jose: Resource.

Vosko, Richard. *Through the Eye of a Rose Window: A Perspective on the Environment for Worship.* San Jose: Resource.

Walden, Carol, ed. *Called to Create: Christian Witness and the Arts.* San Jose: Resource, 1986.

PERIODICALS

Assembly. Notre Dame: Center for Pastoral Liturgy. Five times a year.
Each issue explores the tradition and practice of some aspect of the liturgical event in order to help the community and its ministers enter more deeply into the spirit of the liturgy.

Liturgy. Washington, D.C.: The Liturgical Conference. Quarterly.
Each issue explores a single aspect of liturgy, taking in many disciplines and many church traditions.

Liturgy 90. Chicago: Liturgy Training Publications. Eight times a year.
Features articles on the seasons and sacraments, regular columns on music, environment and art, questions and answers.

Modern Liturgy. San Jose: Resource Publications. Ten times a year.
Devoted exclusively to planning worship for every parish ministry, with help from
all of the arts. Every issue contains ideas for dramas, stories, gestures, songs,
decoration, and design.
Pastoral Music. Washington, D.C.: National Association of Pastoral Musicians.
Six times a year.
Often several major articles on a single theme together with reviews and
announcements. Centers on music but touches on all areas of liturgy.
Worship. Collegeville: The Order of Saint Benedict. Six times a year.
Scholarly journal that since 1926 has been the primary support of liturgical
renewal through the English-speaking world.

PUBLISHER ADDRESSES

Center for Pastoral Liturgy, P.O. Box 81, Notre Dame, IN 46556.
GIA Publications, 7404 South Mason Ave., Chicago, IL 60638.
The Liturgical Conference, 1017 12th St. NW, Washington, DC 20005.
The Liturgical Press, St. John's Abbey, Collegeville, MN 56321.
Liturgy Training Publications, 1800 North Hermitage Ave., Chicago, IL 60622-
1101.
NALR (North American Liturgy Resources), 10802 North 23rd Ave., Phoenix,
AZ 85029.
NPM (National Association of Pastoral Musicians), The Pastoral Press, 225
Sheridan St. NW, Washington, DC 20011.
OCP (Oregon Catholic Press) Publications, 5536 NE Hassalo, Portland, OR
97213.
Paulist Press, 992 Macarthur Blvd., Mahwah, NJ 07403.
Pueblo Publishing Company, 100 West 32nd St., New York, NY 10001-321-.
Resource Publications, 160 East Virginia St. #290, San Jose, CA 95112
Twenty-Third Publications, 185 Willow St., P.O. Box 180, Mystic, CT 06355.
World Library Publications, 3815 North Willow Rd., Schiller Park, IL 60176.

DATE DUE

MAR 2 5 1996			